NEIL LENNON
A Champion's Story

NEIL LENNON

By Mark Henderson

A Champion's Story

Sport Media

Copyright © 2012 Celtic FC Limited

The right of Mark Henderson to be identified as the author of the work has
been asserted by him in accordance with the Copyright, Designs and Patents
Act 1988.

First published in Great Britain in 2012 by Celtic FC Limited.
This edition published in Great Britain in 2012 by Celtic FC Limited.
Designed and produced by Trinity Mirror Sport Media,
PO Box 48, Old Hall Street, Liverpool L69 3EB.

Photographs: Press Association Images,
Scottish News and Sport (SNS)

Printed by CPI Group (UK) Ltd, Croydon, CR0 4YY

ISBN 978 1 908695 27 7

Contents

Acknowledgements

IT was a momentous season as Celtic won the SPL title again. It was Neil Lennon's first league championship as Celtic manager, and it was one that was thoroughly merited. Celtic were the best team in Scotland, scoring more goals than any other team, conceding fewer and having the best disciplinary record in the league.

I was privileged to report on this title-winning season as part of the Celtic multimedia team, and I'm delighted to have been given this opportunity to document the achievement in this book.

First and foremost, I must thank my family – Mum, Dad, Michael and Juliet – for their support, advice and patience, which I have most definitely tested on several occasions!

I am also grateful to everyone in the Celtic multimedia office and particularly to Paul Cuddihy and Joe Sullivan for their encouragement and guidance at every stage of the process.

Finally, I would like to thank Neil Lennon for speaking to me so candidly on a range of subjects which made this all possible, and I wish him continued success in the future.

Mark Henderson
July 2012

Introduction

"...This is just the beginning"

MAY 15, 2011, should have been a day of agony in Paradise. Although Celtic coasted to a 4-0 win over Motherwell, the league championship had been snatched from their grasp by one point. To compound matters, they had been in sight of the finishing line only to stumble, a disastrous 3-2 defeat to Inverness Caledonian Thistle one week earlier ultimately proving fatal to their title aspirations.

For all the progression, stylish football and effort over a breathless twelve months, there would be no championship to celebrate in Neil Lennon's first full season as Celtic manager. Naturally, that was a huge disappointment to the Hoops boss, the players and everyone associated with the club.

Remarkably, there was no funereal atmosphere inside Celtic Park that final day, however. Quite the opposite. Instead, it was a show of solidarity – joyous, stirring and uplifting – as the fans reiterated their backing for the manager and players. It was particularly poignant in the case of the Irishman, given the level of vitriol, physical violence and threats to his life he had endured in one of the most shameful episodes in the Scottish game. That had merely galvanised the Hoops faithful behind the manager, though, and there was a real sense of unity around the club that day.

It was summed up succinctly by the manager on the pitch after the final whistle as he thanked the supporters, promising them that: "This isn't the end… This is just the beginning."

The following weekend, a determined Celtic beat Motherwell 3-0 in the Hampden rain to claim the Scottish Cup. It was the first piece of silverware Neil Lennon had landed since taking the helm, and indeed, the first winner's medal for many of the players in what was a predominantly youthful team. Genuine elation greeted the final whistle and the ensuing celebrations were special. It was the first trophy in just over two years and few could argue Celtic hadn't deserved some reward for their efforts over the course of the campaign.

With the trophy safely back in Paradise, the manager's focus could now switch to fulfilling the promise he made on the pitch one week earlier as preparations for the new season were finalised. Expectations had been heightened among supporters from what they had witnessed from a youthful, exciting team over the previous twelve months and that view was mirrored among the coaching staff. Advancements on all fronts were the objectives. The priority, though, was obvious: the Scottish Premier League title. Absent from the trophy cabinet for three years, and having had it snatched away from their grasp in May, it was the ultimate prize.

"To go one better and win the league," said the manager of his targets. "We had come agonisingly close but to me that had far overstretched my expectations of that season in terms of taking the league all the way and getting to the two cup finals as well. So in terms of this year, it was to go one better and win the championship, progress as far as we could in the cups again and also try and make inroads into Europe because we felt that we had players who were capable of performing well at European level, too."

Those tasked with that responsibility were still relatively young but were now well-practiced in the pressures of representing Celtic.

"We were looking for improvements from last season but we went forward with hope and looking forward to the future," he said. "It was a young squad but very, very talented. I brought a lot of young players to the club, into a different environment and a different culture. They fitted in very well and I wanted to see the job through for them, more than anyone else."

Pain, frustration and regret from the failure lingered from throwing away the championship. It would fuel the desire for redemption.

"It was a great motivation for the players," explained the Irishman. "They were probably a bit sore at the end of the season but they finished on a real high by winning the cup and they got a taste of silverware – and once you've got a taste of it, you want a bit more. Psychologically, it was important to put a trophy in the cabinet for the club.

"The question was: could I, the backroom staff and the players handle the expectations that were going to grow, but that's the challenge which lay in front of us. That's what all our focus was going into the new season."

Here is Neil Lennon's story of that season...

Starting Over

A FINE line exits between success and failure in football. Proper preparation can make the difference, making pre-season a pivotal period for any team harbouring ambitions of winning silverware. There is plenty of historical evidence. The Lisbon Lions often point to Celtic's six-week expedition to the United States in the summer of 1966 as the staging post for a season of unprecedented glory. Not only was it successful on the pitch, sowing the seeds of the attacking, adventurous football which swept all aside in Scotland and Europe, just as significantly, it cultivated a terrific togetherness and team spirit. It was the final piece in Jock Stein's jigsaw, the spark which lit the fuse.

Of course, the scheduling of modern football means such extended tours are now simply impractical. Close seasons have steadily grown shorter and clubs must subsequently strive to secure the same kind of positive outcomes as the Lions within a smaller window of opportunity. Indeed, Scottish football's interlude in summer 2011 was even shorter than normal. The big kick-off had been moved forward to July based on the reasoning that it would aid the Scottish clubs involved in European competition at that early juncture.

This arrangement resulted in a peculiar pre-season schedule for Celtic: the premature season opener with Hibernian would be sandwiched between two layers of four friendly fixtures. It was a predicament Neil Lennon had chewed over since the fixtures for the new campaign were first announced.

Ensuring his team were ready for the game against the Easter Road side swiftly became the immediate target. Once that had been negotiated he would have some breathing space. Until then, Celtic faced a race against the clock. With that in mind, barely four weeks after celebrating the Scottish Cup triumph at Hampden, the manager and his players returned from the briefest of breaks – 24 days – to begin work at Lennoxtown.

The previous year, the manager had taken the team across the Atlantic Ocean for a frenetic four-game tour of North America. This time, Celtic ventured in the opposite direction, spending three weeks in Australia. Three games against A-League opposition were contested in three different cities – Central Coast Mariners (Sydney), Perth Glory (Perth) and Melbourne Victory (Melbourne). Bookending each game was a balanced programme of training, designed to improve fitness and sharpness, while negating the threat of injury. While Stein's side had spent twice as long in America, Australia was still a demanding trip and would consume most of Celtic's precious preparation time. There was a lot riding on it.

"Australia was vital in terms of our preparation for the new season," admitted the manager. "The season started early and we needed to make sure we were ready. There was a lot of travelling and we put in the miles but it was worth it. When we settled in Australia there was plenty of time to recover."

Rustiness, a shortage of match sharpness and tactical experimentation mean little can be gleaned from pre-season results. It doesn't stop some trying, though. Following two defeats on a pre-season tour of North America several years ago, one Scottish tabloid newspaper laughably printed a 'Celts in Crisis' headline accompanied with the customary cracked Celtic crest. Celtic went on to win the championship. It serves as an excellent reminder to not draw conclusions from these early-season friendly fixtures. Still, along with the obvious fitness aims, Neil Lennon quite naturally wanted to see a gradual improvement in performance during the tour of Australia and beyond.

Split into two groups, Celtic arrived in Sydney via Singapore late in June. There was little time to overcome the debilitating effects of jet-lag before the opening game against the Central Coast Mariners, just two days later. Initially, training was light. To clear heads, the squad embarked on a walk around the city centre, past the Opera House, a place which would later be the meeting point for a massive 'Huddle' among the Celtic fans in the lead-up to the match. After one more light session, the team was thrust into action against the Mariners at Sydney's ANZ Stadium, the spectacular arena which hosted the Olympics in 2000. Jaded somewhat from the journey, and with match sharpness still in its infancy, the Hoops served up a commendable display but fell to a narrow 1-0 defeat courtesy of a Troy Hearfield strike late in the game.

"Considering the lack of preparation we had, that was always going to be the toughest game of the tour," said the manager. "The players' condition and the quality, particularly in the second half, meant it was a remarkable performance when you consider the week they had been through. They had been travelling all the way over on Tuesday and

Wednesday and then had one day's training, played very, very well in the second half and controlled the game. The Mariners scored with their one shot on target, and we could've had two penalties, but overall I was delighted with the performance."

Just when Sydney was beginning to feel like home, though, it was time to take to the skies again. Western Australia was the destination. In a part of the world where hitting a six remains more popular than scoring a hat-trick, the team were put through their paces in Perth's historic WACA cricket ground. It was a long way from Craiglang – the fictional council estate from TV show *Still Game* – but celebrity Celt, Paul Riley, who played Winston in the hit BBC comedy, was one interested spectator out of many clad in green and white within the famous old stadium as the players toiled under the Australian sunshine.

The benefits of a full week's training made a marked difference, however, as goals from Gary Hooper and Charlie Mulgrew secured a comfortable 2-0 victory over Perth Glory, who were managed by former Rangers midfielder, Ian Ferguson. It was another step forward.

"Their attitude was very good, the pace they played at and the quality of the play at times was excellent," said the manager. "They had picked up very quickly from where they left off last season, which was very pleasing."

Celtic flew back across the country to round off the tour with a match against Melbourne Victory, regarded as the best-supported club team in the country. In a way, it was a homecoming for Georgios Samaras. His dad was born in the Victorian capital, which houses a large Greek community, and it's a place where he retains many family ties. As a result, he was handed the captain's armband for the match. A smattering of Greek flags and blue and white scarves could be found among the near-capacity crowd at AAMI Park, desperate to see Samaras find the back of the net.

However, it was Scott Brown who eventually broke the home side's resistance in torrential weather conditions, scoring the only goal of the game to ensure the Hoops finished their trip on a high note. Only the heroics of the home side's keeper, Tando Velaphi, prevented Celtic from adding to their tally. Steady improvement on the pitch, togetherness and team spirit strengthened – the manager believed the tour had achieved the main objectives.

"You're always looking for improvement as the tour goes on and we had that. The players looked fitter and sharper. We felt with the close season being so short that they wouldn't have to do a lot of physical work pre-season and it would just be down more to the football side of things. I think it was a good tour. The weather wasn't a problem. I know it was a bit cooler than we would normally expect but we got more work done in that respect because of the lack of humidity. The travelling sounded hectic but it wasn't as bad as people made it out to be. I think the players enjoyed it. You also build that tightness and team spirit, and obviously from a club point of view, you're coming to see the fans in Australia as we have a big fanbase there."

That was one factor which prevailed from the tour of 1966 – bringing the team to a vast ex-pat community. Like many places in the world, there is a sizeable Celtic support in Australia yet, surprisingly, this was only the third time the club had been there, following visits in 1977 and 2009.

As such, interest and excitement had been growing among Antipodean Hoops fans for a long time. From the moment the team landed at Sydney Airport, there was a large presence of Celtic supporters to greet them wherever they ventured. Nearly 60,000 fans attended the three games, while a considerable amount of people also turned out for open training sessions held in each city. Although fitness and conditioning was the main objective, the Hoops boss was keen that his charges, particularly the new recruits, witnessed the reach of the club's worldwide pull.

"I don't think when some players sign they realise how big this club actually is," he said. "The guys who came in the previous summer got a real taste of things in America and it was the same for the new boys in Australia. I knew there were a lot of expats in Australia and that we had a huge following over there but it's always incredible to see so many fans turn out. This club has a huge following around the world.

"We went to Australia to try to make friends. We went there to try to sell the club again and hopefully we played some good football there because it was important to put on a show for the fans that came to see us. And if there were neutrals or those who haven't followed football before as well, we tried to get them to become friends of the club."

As ever, the manager received a rapturous welcome from the fans. He had been keen to reciprocate the gesture along with the players, spending a lengthy period autographing memorabilia and posing for pictures whenever the chance presented itself.

"These fans make unbelievable sacrifices to watch the team play at all hours of the morning, so it was nice to reciprocate that by taking the team out here and letting them see them in the flesh," he said. "They were open sessions and people had come from a long way just to watch it and greet and meet the players. I think they got a kick out of it as much as the players did."

ALTHOUGH Neil Lennon had returned to Glasgow pleased by Celtic's progress and reception Down Under, the amount of travelling had been demanding. He was glad to be home but tired, and that increased his concern about the condition of the players. After all, they had also undergone intense training sessions and taken part in three matches. In a matter of days, Hibernian lay in wait in the Scottish Premier League opener. Would they be ready? It was a nagging worry.

"I was looking forward to getting home after Australia," he said. "The most important thing was trying to avoid long-term injuries and making sure we were ready for Hibs in a fortnight. We did a lot of travelling and from a footballing point of view, we felt it went okay but we were aware that the travelling might have had an effect on the players.

"The travelling was tough but the players also had to go and play, as well as train. It gave us some decent games under our belts, and with the season coming as early as it did we tried to prepare them as best we could."

Rest and recuperation was critical and was certainly factored into the team's preparations for the week ahead. However, undertaking further competitive action was equally important. It takes time to attain match sharpness, so opening the season following such a famine of fixtures was certainly not desirable, and a positive start was vital to preserve the progress of the previous season. Celtic needed games – and fast.

Thankfully, a midweek trip to Championship side, Cardiff City, had been earmarked for that very purpose. The Bluebirds had narrowly failed to earn promotion to the English Premier League the previous season, falling at the play-off stage. Under the direction of former Celt, Malky Mackay, they were expected to mount another serious bid to reach the English top flight, boosted by some shrewd acquisitions in the transfer market. That prediction proved to be correct as they would once again reach the play-off stage at the end of the 2011/12 season. The match was a timely test.

"We just needed another game to give them some more football time so we were pleased we had Cardiff coming up," said the manager.

It was visibly demonstrated by the team selection. There were only three days between the games in the Welsh and Scottish capitals, yet nine of the starting XI would remain the same. A side note to the game concerned Welsh Bhoys, Joe Ledley and Adam Matthews, who returned to their former hunting ground for the first time since moving to Paradise. Both, particularly Ledley, earned a generous reception from the home support, an outcome which isn't always the case in these scenarios.

As it was, a solitary strike from Anthony Stokes gave the Hoops victory in Wales, the Irishman heading home from Emilio Izaguirre's cross. It was a creditable result but, critically, a valuable workout. Neil Lennon hoped it was enough as he knew time was up. Part one of pre-season was over.

EVEN the conditions at Easter Road made it feel like a pre-season game. Bathed in sunshine, with supporters decked out in replica tops and t-shirts, this wasn't a typical image of Scottish football. Think of a biting wind, driving rain and a constant battle to stay warm. No, this felt different. Nonetheless, as normal, three points were at stake and Neil Lennon was desperate for his side to get off to a winning start. Understandably, the tempo was slow in the early stages from both sides but Celtic gradually took control and made the breakthrough courtesy of an accurate finish from Stokes.

The lead may have been slender but the visitors were comfortable, with Lukasz Zaluska enjoying a quiet afternoon between the sticks. In the second half, a fine strike from Ki Sung Yueng ensured the Hoops would start the new campaign with maximum reward. That had been the manager's target since day one of pre-season, and he was thrilled to see his charges accomplish it in such convincing fashion.

"At any time of the year I would've been pleased with that performance but especially because we had only been back a month and hadn't played that much football," he said. "To find that level of performance, particularly in the second half, was very pleasing. Hibs began to tire in the second half because we had the majority of possession so we were able to cut them open.

"There wasn't much in the game before we scored. We were still finding our feet, but we made the breakthrough early and it was a great goal. We had a bit of luck with the goalkeeper making a mistake but Stoksey's touch and finish was excellent. I felt the second goal was coming because we were starting to get bodies forward. Joe Ledley was getting into good positions and Ki found himself outside the box on a couple of occasions."

In the first part of pre-season, Celtic had faced three Australian A-League sides and a team playing in the English Championship. They had helped the players achieve a level of fitness good enough to see off Hibernian. Three points had been safely banked. For his team to be ready for sterner challenges at home and abroad, though, Neil Lennon knew they not only required further game-time but a variety of testing fixtures over the next two weeks. This formed the thinking behind the four remaining matches of pre-season.

It began with the return of a Celtic favourite from the club's centenary season, Mick McCarthy, who brought his Wolves team to Paradise. Many of those who didn't start against Hibs were given an opportunity against the English Premier League side, including Charlie Mulgrew, James Forrest and Victor Wanyama. All three performed excellently and would go on to become integral players over the season. A Jamie O'Hara free-kick and an own goal from Filip Twardzik gave the visitors the spoils, but it was a generally good report card for Celtic.

"There were a lot of positives for me, we created some really good chances and made the goalkeeper work," said the manager. "James Forrest was outstanding in the second half, as was Adam Matthews while Charlie Mulgrew and Victor Wanyama got a game. So there were a lot of good things to come out from the younger players."

Celtic's early exit from Europe the previous season had hurt the Irishman. He passionately believes the Hoops belong on that stage and he was determined to ensure they extended their stay this time around. Celtic's opener in the Dublin Super Cup against Inter Milan was a valuable opportunity to hone the team's European experience before the real action got underway. The encounter with the Italian giants evoked memories of the Lisbon Lions' European Cup triumph in 1967, but the manager's main concern was to its future benefits and he used the chance to experiment tactically with the Europa League in mind.

"It was a fantastic opportunity for us and the players as well, to gauge where we were in comparison with teams of the calibre of Inter Milan," he said. "It gave us an opportunity to look at a different formation and different personnel in different positions to see if we could adapt to that against a real quality of opposition. At a club like ours, not just domestic football is important.

"The success we had in the last decade showed how much European football means to the club financially and to the fans emotionally. The fans don't demand it but they expect it. We felt Europe was important, not just for the club but the players and the backroom staff, including myself, as part of our development."

Celtic supporters from all across the Emerald Isle flocked to the recently-constructed Aviva Stadium in Dublin to take in the game. Certainly, they were entertained. The game was compelling viewing. But it was Inter who came out on top thanks to first-half efforts from Luc Castaignos and Giampolo Pazzini. Brazilian, Thiago Motta, saw red for the Serie A side as tempers boiled over. This was no friendly. Although defeat had been the outcome, the manager believed it showed that many of his charges were well-equipped for the big stage.

"The majority of the players could compete at a very good level, and a very high level," he said. "We just needed a little tweaking here and a little bit more understanding in the back four at times. But in terms of our play in general, against quality opposition in Inter Milan, we did very well. I felt we played very well in the game overall and, but for a bit of luck and some good goalkeeping, the scoreline could have been different. I wanted to put an extra midfield player in but I couldn't do that with the personnel we had on the day, so we just went with a different formation to what we had in mind to play with, and it came across okay. We adopted an approach where we wanted Shaun Maloney just to play in the hole a little bit and leave Georgios Samaras up front, as he likes that role and stretches teams quite well.

"Again, but for a bit of luck he could've had a hat-trick in the first half. He made the keeper make two really good saves and got under a cross for a header which he probably should've done better with, but I was pleased with his contribution. I wanted us to compete at that level and do better at times. There was obviously room for improvement but on the evidence of the first game I wasn't overly unhappy, just disappointed by the result."

Celtic concluded the tournament with a resounding 5-0 triumph over an Irish League XI. Gary Hooper and Stokes both bagged braces, while Daryl Murphy was also on target. It was a comfortable win. The main highlight was the prolific form of the two main goalscorers of the previous campaign – Hooper and Stokes.

"The two of them came on against Inter for half-an-hour and did well and they did very well in the second half against the Irish League Select," he said. "So I was pleased with those two and I know what I get from them. You can never say they guarantee goals because there is no such thing in football but they create plenty of chances and they seem to like playing alongside each other and they are both good finishers. So it was nice to see them score some good goals. In the second game we were sloppy in the first half, but in the second half we were a lot better and a lot more like ourselves."

Following the trip to Ireland, the final chance to fine-tune match sharpness came against Premier League newcomers, Swansea City.

Celtic had their opportunities in Wales but it was the hosts who took the spoils through second-half strikes from Angel Rangel and Stephen Dobbie. It was the fourth game in the space of seven days – a hectic schedule – but the manager had taken account of the fatigue factor.

"I had tried to balance things off with not over-exerting them with the games and was just trying to keep as many of them fresh for Aberdeen as we could."

Pre-season had drawn to a close. It was a necessary exercise but there was a sense of relief and anticipation at the resumption of normal service. From now on, Celtic would be fighting for tangible reward. Only now could the success of the past eight weeks be measured.

"I think the players were looking forward to that competitive edge again in the games," said the manager. "We had needed the games – we needed to work on a few things and needed some players to get some game-time. And they were worthwhile. We made a decent start to the season."

NEIL LENNON oversaw a major revamp of Celtic's squad in his first summer in charge. The main structure had been put in place. At the start of the 2011/12 season, his task was adding the finishing touches. Over the course of the previous campaign, a host of young players from countries across the world had fused together to produce one of the most exhilarating Hoops teams of recent years. Ultimately, they had fallen just short of lifting the title in their first season together.

They were only expected to improve into a new campaign. On the whole, the manager was content with his existing pool of players while recognising several areas which required strengthening. The defence had already been bolstered by the start of pre-season, with the signings of Kelvin Wilson and Adam Matthews, who arrived on pre-contract agreements from Nottingham Forest and Cardiff City, respectively.

Wilson had been a long-term target of the manager, who had first spotted the central defender's talents at first-hand during his playing spell at the City Ground. Matthews was rated as one of the most promising young players in Wales and had been linked with moves to clubs, including Manchester United. His capture was regarded as a coup. Both made a favourable early impressions, and would feature regularly throughout the campaign. Victor Wanyama was confirmed as the club's third acquisition of the summer during the tour of Australia, joining from Belgian outfit, Beerschot AC. Few had heard of the young Kenyan internationalist at the time. It would prove a wonderful piece of business.

"We had a great nucleus and a great base of the squad," explained the manager. "We had already added Kelvin and Adam to that on pre-contracts. With Victor coming in we improved the squad as well. I felt it was a young squad but on the experience of the game the previous year it would be good to go.

"We were looking for a centre-half and that's where we brought Kelvin in. We felt Victor was a real talent and we thought it would be folly of us not to take him – we knew what we were getting. We knew it might take him a little bit of time to settle into the country and the culture but he had a fantastic season for us."

In the last line of defence, there was also a towering gap to plug. Fraser Forster had been one of the successes of the previous year during his season-long loan spell from Newcastle United. Together with Lukasz Zaluska, who played in the first two SPL matches of 2010/11, the Englishman helped Celtic to twenty-three clean sheets in the league, beating the club record which had been set in 2001/02.

Although he had returned to Tyneside on completion of his Hoops deal, both parties remained keen on concluding a new arrangement. At times, it seemed the deal wouldn't come to fruition, and several other shot-stoppers were strongly linked with a move to Celtic, including Croatian internationalist, Stipe Pletikosa, who played two matches as a trialist. As the season kicked off, Celtic had yet to recruit another keeper. Forster was always the Hoops boss' prime target for the position, though, and a season-long loan was finally rubber-stamped on the eve of Celtic's Europa League clash with FC Sion. Patience and perseverance had paid off.

"There were areas we needed to strengthen and we were waiting on Fraser coming back to us again on loan from Newcastle, so things were a little bit unsure – as they always are pre-season – as to whether we were going to get the players we wanted or not," said the manager. "But thankfully Fraser came on board and we were delighted with that. We worked hard in the background to try and bring him in and we eventually did that so we were very, very pleased. I always felt we would get a keeper. Fraser was the one who was top of the list. There were other options that we could have gone for but we were thrilled that he came."

Bringing in a striker to complement the existing frontmen at the club was also a key objective and speculation linked the club with several names over the summer. On August 30, one day before the transfer window slammed shut, the manager was successful in that aim as the signing of Mohamed Bangura on a four-year deal from AIK Stockholm was confirmed. The Sierra Leonean came highly recommended with a glowing appraisal from Henrik Larsson no less. Aged twenty-three, he fitted into the transfer policy adopted by the club in recent years, which targeted youth and potential. However, injury would blight his first campaign in Scotland.

"We didn't get Mo until the end of the transfer window. He came highly recommended by people in the Swedish game. We had him watched for a year or so, and all the reports were very positive."

In normal circumstances, that may have concluded the manager's summer recruitment drive. He had reinforced several areas in the side

– his intention at the start – but he was forced to rethink his plans following Emilio Izaguirre's horror injury in early August. Scotland's Player of the Year, a crucial cog in the Celtic machine both defensively and offensively, broke his ankle after falling awkwardly in the league game at Pittodrie. He would subsequently miss six months of the season, a huge blow. Finding an equal replacement for such a gifted individual was impossible but the manager knew he needed to at least boost his options at left-back.

With hours of the transfer window remaining, the loan signing of experienced Moroccan internationalist, Badr El Kaddouri, from Dynamo Kiev was announced. With over forty caps for his country, and having spent nine years at the Ukrainian giants, he seemed to fit the bill as someone who could hit the ground running in Scottish football. He also possessed an instinct for attacking – a vital commodity in Celtic full-backs. However, the consistency of Charlie Mulgrew would limit his first-team appearances.

Invariably, a number of players departed in the opposite direction. Heading out on season-long loans were Daryl Murphy (Ipswich Town) and Richie Towell (Hibernian). Both Jos Hooiveld and Morten Rasmussen also exited on six-month loan spells to Southampton and Sivasspor, respectively.

Shaun Maloney, meanwhile, ended his second spell in Paradise by making the move to the English Premier League with Wigan Athletic, where he teamed up with his former Hoops team-mate, Gary Caldwell. He had made a total of one hundred and seven-six appearances for Celtic, scoring fifty-two goals.

Perhaps the greatest achievement of the summer transfer activity, though, was the retention of essential members of the side. Having worked so assiduously to build a team over the previous twelve months, the last thing the manager wanted was to see it break apart.

However, success attracts attention, and it was natural there were vultures circling some of Celtic's high-profile players on the back of their impact over the previous term. It was a period of uncertainty for the whole management team. Ultimately, reported interest in the likes of Gary Hooper and Beram Kayal was staved off by the club and the manager went forward with his blueprint for success still intact.

Slowing Down

IT may well be a marathon rather than a sprint, yet every football manager seeks to hit the ground running at the start of the season. Early momentum can develop into an unstoppable force. It creates belief, confidence and togetherness – crucial components for any side with designs on success.

In his first full season at the helm, Neil Lennon guided his newly-assembled side to nine successive domestic wins at the start of the campaign. It was a remarkable achievement at the time, particularly for a team that was still gelling, providing the impetus for the remainder of the season. Repeating that feat in his second season would always be a tough mission, but the manager hoped for a similar outcome.

An opening-day win at Hibernian had been an excellent start and Celtic's second game on the cards would be another difficult away assignment, this time to Aberdeen. The four friendlies squeezed between both fixtures made it feel like the league race was now truly underway. The Hoops appeared to have reaped the benefits of further match practice since the trip to Easter Road as they quickly gained control of proceedings at Pittodrie, displaying a greater urgency. Anthony Stokes' second-half strike proved enough to secure a second successive SPL victory. In truth, the winning margin should have been greater but for some profligacy on Celtic's part.

"We certainly deserved to win the game at Pittodrie and if we had a little bit more cutting edge we would have won more comfortably," said the manager. "We gained control of the game, and our passing and movement was excellent. We always thought that if we had got the first goal early enough then the game would open up and we'd have more and more opportunities to score."

The Hoops boss should have cut a contented figure as he headed down the A90 back to Glasgow – two difficult away fixtures had been successfully negotiated, while the 100 per cent league record remained intact. But genuine concern over Emilio Izaguirre's broken ankle, sustained innocuously during the first half, was at the forefront of his mind and in the thoughts of the players. Losing such an influential member of the side so early in the season was undoubtedly a significant blow. The mood was solemn.

"It was a huge blow, first of all for the player himself - that was my main concern," said the manager. "It was also a huge blow for the team because he was such an important player for us over the last year. He brought great quality so it was going to be hard to find a replica of that very quickly."

As the Honduran internationalist prepared for a lengthy spell on the treatment table, Celtic had to readjust, refocus and move on. Dundee United were in town for the first SPL match at Paradise, and the importance of earning a positive result had been drummed home to the players by the Irishman.

Successful in restoring the 'thunder' to Celtic Park the previous season, the manager was anxious to maintain that positive, uplifting atmosphere in the stadium by continuing to serve up entertaining fare on the pitch.

His players responded to that call, producing some sparkling football in a resounding 5-1 win over United. Stokes and Johnny Russell traded goals before Gary Hooper's header put Celtic in charge at the break. After the restart, the hosts upped the tempo, with Ki Sung Yueng, Joe Ledley and James Forrest all on target. The home supporters departed in high spirits.

"It was our first home game, so again it was very important to get off to a good start, get the supporters' backing and allow them to see the type of football which the team was trying to play," said the manager. "It was important that the team won the game and maintained a one hundred per cent record. Dundee United are one of the better, more consistent teams in the division. They are very dangerous opponents and they took points off us at home the previous year, so to win and play as well we did was obviously very pleasing, considering the lack of preparation we had going into the game.

"For five different guys to score the five goals was great, and our all-round game was also excellent. Lukasz Zaluska had to make a couple of good saves at important times, but overall I was pleased. We had plenty of possession the week before against Aberdeen, we created good chances but we weren't as clinical so I got everything in that aspect."

Barring the loss of Izaguirre, it had been a perfect start to the season, with a maximum nine points accrued, and a buoyant Celtic now switched their attention to the first European test of the season as Swiss outfit FC Sion arrived in Glasgow for the first leg of the Europa League qualifier at Paradise.

Off-field matters had dominated pre-match discussions, centring on the Swiss side's alleged infringement of a transfer ban, imposed by FIFA in the previous year for inducing Egyptian goalkeeper, Essam

El-Hadary, to break his contract. During the summer, claiming the sanction had ended, Sion signed several new players, including former Celtic trialist Pascal Feindouno and former Hearts defender, Jose Goncalves. FIFA, backed by UEFA, warned of sanctions if any of these ineligible players were fielded in European competition.

The ensuing uncertainty in the days before the game over which team Laurent Rousseay would select was far from ideal for the Celtic manager as he attempted to finalise his preparations and set his side out accordingly. It was only when the teams were announced prior to kick-off that the ambiguity was removed: Sion had failed to heed the threat and included the banned players in their side. Their fate would be decided later.

Among the Celtic starting XI, it was notable who was absent. Hooper was ruled out because of a sprained ankle and his predatory presence in the box would be missed as the Bhoys endured a frustrating night in Paradise. The visitors' goal was threatened on several occasions, chiefly through Charlie Mulgrew, Kris Commons and Shaun Maloney, but the breakthrough remained elusive. The match would finish goalless, not a terrible outcome but it left an uphill task for the second leg.

"Our play in the final third was poor," said the manager. "The chances we did create were decent ones that we should have had somebody on the end of. We missed some really good chances."

It was the first blotch on a perfect canvas but others would soon appear. Three days later, Celtic hosted St Johnstone for their third home game in the space of a week. While the Hoops had already plundered eight league goals, the Perth Saints had found that part of the game elusive and had still to break their duck in 2011/12. Unfortunately for Celtic, this was the game where the visitors managed to add a scoring touch to their defensive doggedness.

Left to rue a number of squandered opportunities, the Hoops fell to their first reversal of the campaign, courtesy of a deflected shot from Dave Mackay in the second half. Commons had been presented with the best chance in the third minute from the penalty spot but was thwarted by Saints' keeper Peter Enckelman. He also struck the post with a free-kick. Unfortunately it was a common affliction among the entire team as several terrific chances were spurned, allowing Mackay's goal to prove decisive. The 100 per cent record was gone.

"We weren't clinical enough," said the manager. "There was a wee bit of that in our play at the time and it was two games where we didn't score at home which was very rare for us. I could have put that down to concentration and quality but whatever it was, we had hit the post a couple of times and were missing simple chances. We were snatching at things and maybe we didn't deserve the result we got but if you don't take your chances, that's what happens in football.

"We missed clear-cut chances, we were complacent in front of goal and wasteful, and the longer the game goes on at 0-0 you give the opposition encouragement. We dominated the game and St Johnstone scored with one of their only attacks but that happens in football. It was disappointing as we didn't see it coming because we felt the team was strong and good enough to win the game. It was a setback for us."

Defeat to St Johnstone was certainly not ideal preparation as Celtic sought to salvage their European dream in the second leg of the play-off with FC Sion. A reaction was required – and so were bodies. Deprived of Gary Hooper, Beram Kayal and Kelvin Wilson for the visit of the Perth outfit, there was hope they would recover from their respective knocks in time for the match. Charlie Mulgrew was another doubt. He had started against the Saints but had been forced to leave the fray because of a hamstring injury.

The Alpine setting of Sion, with its lush valleys and snow-covered peaks, was picturesque – but Celtic couldn't afford to be distracted by the surroundings. Finding the back of the net would be necessary for the team and the Irishman knew an improvement would be required in that department.

"I just wanted them to put their chances away," he said. "Goals change games – the psychology of the games. We had been pleased with their overall play. It was just that a cutting edge had been lacking in the previous two games but I had no worries that it would come back very soon."

As kick-off approached, the skies darkened, heralding the arrival of torrential rain and thunder and lightning. If it was a sign that events were not going to go in Celtic's favour, then it was unerringly accurate. Less than a minute of the match had elapsed before they found themselves a man and a goal down as Daniel Majstorovic saw red for a foul on Guilherme Afonso inside the box. Feindouno duly converted the spot-kick.

It was a nightmare start. The 10 men valiantly fought on, holding out until the 63rd minute when Feindouno doubled his, and his side's tally. Although Mulgrew rifled home from a free-kick 12 minutes from time to hand the Hoops a lifeline, Sion added a third on the counter-attack to extinguish the faint hopes that still existed. It's challenging enough to earn a result on the continent, but losing a goal and a player so early in the match made Celtic's task almost impossible. Frustrated, the manager did, however, extract some solace from his players' character in the face of adversity.

"I was very disappointed," he said. "We gave ourselves a lot to do after two or three minutes. We had emphasised that we needed to start the game well, but after that I thought we played very well. Even when the second goal went in, the players more than anybody else felt they were still in the tie and got the goal.

"We felt then we were going to get the result we wanted, and we shot ourselves in the foot for the third goal. I was very disappointed but there was still a lot I took out of the game in terms of chances created and the attitude of the players – they never let their heads go down. Even at 2-0, they kept going and I thought we deserved better out of the game. There were some very good performances."

In the space of a week, Celtic's perfect start to the season had disintegrated. Three wins had been followed by a draw and two defeats. The early momentum had come to a shuddering halt. What could have caused such a dramatic stutter in form?

"I think the loss of Emilio made us rethink the defence as well, as we had plans in place for him to have a big season for us again," reflected the manager. "Because the games came so early in the season, players were still finding their feet and we were still finding what the best team was for a particular run of games. We didn't find any cohesive sort of performances for a month or two after that."

NEIL LENNON had endured a difficult seven days but at this stage it was still just a setback. A visit to St Mirren Park would provide Celtic with a quick opportunity of redemption to arrest the poor run of form. There was also a welcome fillip ahead of the game with the news that Izaguirre and Mulgrew had both penned new long-term deals, which would see them remain at the club until at least 2015.

On the field, there was further encouragement as Celtic shrugged off the disappointment of the Sion result to earn a creditable three points over a Saints side who had started the season in confident fashion. The visitors started with purpose and, although an early strike from Stokes was harshly chalked off for a foul, a quick-fire double from Hooper gave Celtic a two-goal lead inside the first 15 minutes. It was an advantage they maintained for the rest of the game, despite the best efforts of the home side.

It was a timely win, reducing some of the pressure which had been building on the Bhoys while keeping them in contention at the SPL summit as a two-week hiatus for international football got under-way. League duty resumed with a home fixture against a high-flying Motherwell team who went into the match above Celtic in the league, albeit having played one game more.

There was a hasty turnaround for those returning from national service, with many players arriving back in Glasgow within forty-eight hours of the kick-off. Notwithstanding those who returned nursing knocks, it was hardly ideal preparation for what seemed a potentially tricky encounter. However, on the whole, the manager went into the match filled with optimism.

"We were looking forward to it," he said. "It had been a good break for the backroom staff and the players who weren't away on interna-tional duty. They were quite fresh and we went into this one on the back of a good result at St Mirren. We were hoping to improve on that performance against a Motherwell team who had started the season very well. I had watched them twice myself and they beat Inverness comfortably on the opening day of the season. They were very good going forward against Dunfermline in their previous game and they had players in form."

Motherwell, however, were no match for a rampant Celtic, who showed no ill-effects from the international week to run out 4-0 winners, wiping out the memories of the previous home defeat to St Johnstone. The outstanding James Forrest put the hosts in front with a wonderfully-worked goal, before Joe Ledley doubled the advantage before half-time. A 30-yard strike from Ki and Forrest's second of the afternoon sealed the points for the dominant Celts. It was the complete performance – sparkling football, goals and a clean sheet.

"It was the best we had played so far," said the manager. "I was delighted by the manner of the performance, the result and the four goals – I thought they were great goals as well. It was important we won, and important we played well on the back of the St Johnstone defeat at home. I think the fans had responded to that. There was some good, entertaining football. I thought we were dynamic at times, particularly on the counter-attack.

"It was still early in the season to start putting down markers but that was more like us. It was the form we showed consistently the previous year, and I was delighted with the performance. Everyone made a positive contribution, even the substitutes who came on made us better. So I was thrilled with the performance."

While it had been an impressive all-round display, Forrest was the star of the show. Constantly tormenting the visitors with his explosive pace and movement, he also took his goals with some aplomb. It was only the 20-year-old's second start of the season, but from this moment on, he was one of the first names on the team sheet.

"He was superb," said the manager. "We had tried to break him in lightly as he was prone to picking up little niggling injuries. That was only his second start of the season but it was the best performance I had seen from him, and I had known him a while. He's a player who can play either side or through the middle and is exciting as well, and has a goal in him. You saw all his qualities. He was exceptional. I just saw an improvement in him all the time."

Seemingly back on track domestically, Celtic could now return to the European arena with renewed confidence and belief. The Hoops had been restored to the Europa League at the expense of Sion following a decision of UEFA's Control and Disciplinary Body, who deemed that the Swiss side had breached its rules in both ties.

Celtic entered a group alongside Atletico Madrid, Rennes and Udinese – demanding yet mouth-watering ties. The Hoops' first game would be away to Atletico. Farcically, the Sion president, Christian Constantin, claimed his side would also travel to the Spanish capital to play the game. It turned out to be bluster.

Matters could now return to the football and Celtic recognised they would face an almighty task in the Vicente Calderon Stadium against the big-spending Spaniards. Not for the first time on their travels, the Hoops made a poor start as Columbian hitman, Falcao, struck for the hosts from a corner in the third minute. However, Celtic recovered gamely from the early blow and nearly restored parity following a swift counter-attack, which Hooper was unable to finish off. Brazilian mid-fielder, Diego, sealed the points for the home side in the second half to end hopes of a comeback. Nonetheless, it was a commendable display to open the group phase.

It had been an exerting night's endeavour in Madrid and there was little chance to recover before the first Glasgow derby of the season at Ibrox. At this early juncture in the campaign there was little to separate the two sides, with Rangers going into the game holding a slender one-point advantage. With so many fixtures still to fulfil, it was never going to be a title-deciding match. Not that any further incentive was required for either side, though. A full-blooded, frenetic and passionate contest is always guaranteed during these duels, regardless of wider circumstances. Scott Brown handed a pre-match boost to the Bhoys by taking his place in the starting XI. His energy, determination and drive are always vital in these keenly-contested encounters. Six goals and one sending off later, it was over.

The hosts struck first through a Steven Naismith goal. Parity was restored when Hooper fastened on to Brown's precise pass and expertly finished into the far corner, and Celtic went in ahead at the break when Allan McGregor fumbled Badr El Kaddouri's drive into the net. After the interval, though, the Hoops' fortunes took a tumble. Brown, a major influence in the first half, went off with an ankle injury – his final involvement for several months – while Charlie Mulgrew was ordered off after receiving a second yellow card. Goals from Nikica Jelavic, Kyle Lafferty and Naismith turned the match around. It had been a disastrous forty-five minutes and, significantly, Celtic now trailed their city rivals by four points.

"I wasn't happy and I'm sure the supporters weren't happy either," said the manager. "We had a grip of the game and we let it go so that was a huge disappointment."

Following two wins over St Mirren and Motherwell, two defeats in the space of four days had brought Celtic crashing back down to earth. A worrying pattern was emerging.

THE aftermath of a derby defeat is never a pleasant experience, and the reversal in mid-September was no different. Wallowing in dejection wasn't an option for Neil Lennon and his players. Once the post-mortem had been conducted, the errors highlighted and some forth-right views exchanged, the focus was on returning to winning ways against Ross County in the fourth round of the Scottish Communities League Cup.

The Highlanders were already riding high in the First Division at that point and would go on to win the league with some ease. It was a tie laced with potential pitfalls. County's shock 2-0 win over Celtic in the Scottish Cup semi-final just 18 months earlier remained a vivid and painful memory.

Factor in the small pitch, a ground packed to the rafters and a traditional cup-tie atmosphere, then the tie transformed into a major obstacle. In torrential conditions, it soon transpired that the pre-match predictions had proven accurate as both sides fought for supremacy. However, Celtic displayed a clinical edge to take the lead from their first attack through Gary Hooper's close-range effort.

To their credit, the hosts didn't submit but once Scott Boyd turned Stokes' delivery into his own net seven minutes after the break, the Hoops never looked in danger of surrendering their two-goal advantage. The manager could even afford to hand Irish teenager,

Paul George, his first-team bow in the closing stages with the winger nearly capping off a memorable evening, only to be denied by home shot-stopper, Michael Fraser. Regardless, Celtic were through to the last eight of the competition.

"I had got the reaction I wanted from the players," said the Hoops boss. "The attitude was a lot better, the work-rate off the ball was a lot better and our play in general was a lot better. It was a small step in the right direction. We weren't getting carried away obviously but we were pleased with the clean sheet as well, and on the counter-attack we could have added to the scoreline.

"I couldn't ask any more from the players. Obviously they were disappointed and we had to pick them up. We got the early goal and that settled us. It was difficult and you are always looking to see what character they had and they showed that, and there were some good individual performances from Mulgrew and Ledley."

One black spot from the match was a knock sustained by Kelvin Wilson, which saw him substituted at the interval. Further investigation later revealed the defender had suffered an injury to his Achilles tendon, meaning he would be absent for up to eight weeks. Celtic's injury list was mounting.

Having suffered two defeats from their first seven matches in the league, it was imperative that Celtic picked up maximum points when they returned to SPL action for the visit of Inverness Caley Thistle. Now trailing Rangers by four points, the Hoops knew they could ill-afford many more slip-ups and allow the gap to increase. It was the first time Celtic had faced Terry Butcher's side since the 3-2 league defeat the previous May, the game which struck a fatal blow to the Hoops' title bid.

"It was the first league game after the Rangers match, so it was important for the players to put their case across very strongly," said the manager. "We just had to win the game. It was a simple remit we had going into every game – try and win it, and try and win it well. We had to try and get the fans re-energised again. So the home form had to be important for us."

Denied the services of Brown, Kelvin Wilson and Commons through injury, and Charlie Mulgrew through suspension, the manager was able to call upon Georgios Samaras, Mark Wilson, Paddy McCourt and Thomas Rogne, who had all returned to contention following the game in Dingwall.

After a slow start, Celtic suddenly sprang into life just before the half-hour mark, scoring two quick-fire goals to ruthlessly punish the Highlanders. Ledley opened Celtic's account with a crisp drive from distance, before Forrest continued his rich vein of form by fastening on to Ki's raking pass and sweeping a shot into the far corner. They proved to be the two moments of real quality in the game as Celtic held out comfortably for a valuable three points.

"They were great goals and I was very pleased with the individual performances from the two goalscorers," said the Hoops boss. "Ledley was playing very well and Forrest was excellent. The performances of Kayal and Ki in midfield were also pleasing. We got better as the game went on and were in control. Without being brilliant, it was a very good result.

"At times we had been wasteful in possession. It wasn't by any means a vintage performance, but it was solid enough. We relied on a very good midfield performance but that happens. They can turn a game in an instant. It was a great clean sheet and three points under difficult circumstances. Sometimes you've just got to grind these out so I was very, very pleased."

Celtic had recovered from the two reversals to grind out two wins. Nonetheless, it had been a stuttering start. The key now was taking this winning form into European competition and building some sustained momentum for the weeks and months ahead. Atletico had been a demanding start, but Udinese promised to be just as severe a test. Unbeaten in Serie A, Francesco Guidolin's side were organised, defensively strong and packed with pace, and in their talisman, Italian internationalist Antonio Di Natale, they also possessed one of the most lethal striking talents in European football. However, Celtic held home advantage and were confident of pulling off a good result.

"We wanted to be positive and try and take the game to Udinese, who were a class side," said the manager. "We had them watched three times and they were a brilliant counter-attacking team as well, as we saw against Arsenal [in the Champions League qualifiers]. They were one of the best sides in Serie A and were full of danger but, being the home team, we wanted to try and take the game to them if we could."

Another factor in Celtic's favour would be the vocal backing of the Paradise crowd.

"It lifts the players' performances and it lifts the team as a whole. Getting that unity around the stadium is fantastic," added the Hoops boss. "A lot of them were new to this. It's an experience they hadn't had before. We had a touch of it in the Sion game when the atmosphere was great and there had been a good atmosphere against Inverness."

The Celtic fans were given something to cheer in the third minute as Ki swept Celtic in front from the penalty spot following a foul on Hooper. Just as it seemed that Celtic were about to deservedly collect their first win of group, though, the visitors were awarded a spot-kick in the closing stages when Hooper was penalised for brushing against Udinese's Neuton in the box. It was a harsh decision, but Almen Abdi made no mistake from twelve yards.

"We had to win our home games and if it wasn't for that decision we would have won that night," said the manager, "but we were still playing the right way."

Nonetheless, encouraged by the display against Udinese, he believed there were reasons to be optimistic as he geared up for Celtic's next league fixture which would be at the testing venue of Tynecastle.

"We had played well against Udinese and we deserved to win," he said. "But we hadn't really hit the heights yet that we know we're capable of. I thought it was only a matter of time before we did though."

The weekend visit to the capital wasn't to be the occasion. Celtic squandered several decent openings in the first half and were punished after the break as goals from Rudi Skacel and Ryan Stevenson gave Hearts the points. The Hoops' misery was compounded by Kris Commons' red card.

"We should have been coming in at the break a goal or two up so we told them to go and kill the game off in the first ten or fifteen minutes of the second half," said the manager. "Again we were in control but we didn't really test the goalkeeper enough for my liking. I didn't see a 2-0 defeat coming at half-time. I thought we were solid. I thought we passed the ball well but I was disappointed by our play in the final third. It should have been a lot better with the quality of players we had on the pitch.

"We weren't clinical enough and that was the biggest disappointment. We were wasteful in front of goal and away from home, the longer the game is goal-less, you give the opposition encouragement. We missed simple, clear-cut chances and if we had got a goal we might have gone on to win the game comfortably, but the first goal changed the nature of the game."

The defeat left Celtic in third place and ten points behind Rangers, with one game in hand. It was a real low point. The pressure on the team was now mounting.

"We had to find more consistency in our performances. We had already lost three games and the previous season we only lost four. It was a difficult position I was in but I understood that. The players were going to have to turn it around, and I was going to have to turn it around. I had a lot of thinking to do. I could have maybe changed the formation if it wasn't working or certainly the personnel anyway, but I wasn't making excuses – the team was strong enough to win. We had a game in hand but we had to win that and cut it to seven and eat away at it. The gap was redeemable but I wasn't going to pull the wool over anybody's eyes. We couldn't afford to lose games."

The statistics were telling. After starting the season with three successive victories, Celtic had won only four of their next eleven games in all competitions, threatening to leave them an insurmountable distance behind the leaders in early October, so much so that some foolishly declared the title race over.

CELTIC simply hadn't managed to achieve a consistently high standard of performance in the early part of the season, and Neil Lennon would never attempt to deny that fact. However, there were mitigating factors for the fluctuation in form which must be mentioned. New players were still settling into the side while Celtic had been wasteful in front of goal on several occasions, failing to translate their dominance into points. Injuries, however, had been a constant curse.

Key personnel were frequently consigned to the treatment table for both short and long-term spells, denying the manager consistency in selection and the opportunity to discover his strongest starting XI. On a regular basis, he was forced to deploy players in unfamiliar positions and ask them to carry out a role they weren't accustomed to. It was a major headache.

"At one point we had eleven players out, which is a team, and that would affect any side no matter who the manager is or who the club is," the Hoops boss said. "It was a case of re-jigging the team almost every week. You were trying to stitch a team together, and maybe that was why we weren't getting the consistency that we wanted. It was very disruptive as you are chopping and changing the team all the time and sometimes you are putting square pegs in round holes and just hoping they get by. But we did okay. We got through the rough period and once we started seeing the boys coming back to full fitness, and finding that level of consistency we were looking for, we just felt we were going to be alright then.

"In the league games we were okay to start off with, and again at the start of the season you are always looking to see what your best team is, and in the second game of the season we lost Emilio to a serious injury. That set us back in terms of what we wanted to do as he was such a pivotal player for us the previous season and we had to rethink the structure of the squad."

While this was the most noteworthy injury in this part of the season, it was by no means the last. Another lengthy absentee was Scott Brown. The captain missed nearly three months of the campaign with an ankle injury, which he initially picked up on international duty. A figurehead for the team and a driving presence in the midfield, he was the type of player who could be relied upon in times of adversity, and there were plenty instances of that around this juncture.

"We lost Scott and he had to have the surgery," said the Hoops boss. "We knew he wasn't right anyway. You could just tell by the way he was running that he just wasn't himself. We had a couple of other ones along the way, people picking up injuries here and there and we had to keep changing the back four and obviously Emilio was out for such a concerted period of time as well."

The defensive department was particularly plagued by injuries. At one point, the situation was so dire the manager joked that 71-year-old club legend, Billy McNeill, was the only player fit for selection! No-one was immune. Kelvin Wilson had been a mainstay in the defence since joining the club from Nottingham Forest in the summer until his

Achilles injury picked up at Ross County in mid-September.

"It was a huge blow," admitted the manager. "We already had Emilio Izaguirre out and Cha Du-Ri was out for another few weeks. It just meant we had to re-jig things a little bit again in defence."

Norwegian centre-half, Thomas Rogne, only made his first appearance of the season at the end of October. His progress would be hampered until the festive period. Mark Wilson, another fixture in the back-four during the previous season, rarely figured after October, in part because of his recurring knee problem. Glenn Loovens and Cha Du-Ri's participation were also restricted by knocks and only Daniel Majstorovic, Charlie Mulgrew and Adam Matthews remained largely injury-free at this stage. This was hardly conducive to assembling a solid defence.

At the other end of the park, Kris Commons, a vital member of the team the previous season, was blighted by a series of niggling injuries, while summer signing, Mo Bangura, would also require to go under the knife with a knee problem. There was no underlying reason for this plague of knocks, niggles and broken bones other than pure bad luck. With the backing of Celtic's top-class medical department, headed by Dr Roddy Macdonald, they all made a full recovery and contributed to the team's success. The medical team's function at the club couldn't be underestimated, according to the manager.

"They play a huge role and I think we have made big improvements in that area over the two years in terms of the rehabilitation and in terms of minimising the injuries. But there is very little you can do with trauma injuries – injuries that are picked up on the pitch through collisions," he said.

"We have been able to deal a lot better with soft tissue injuries like hamstrings and groins, we have been able to deal with that a lot better as we had a spell there a couple of years ago when we had four or five out with hamstrings and two or three injured them again, so we have been able to avoid that and a lot of that is down to Roddy, Tim Williamson and the rest of the team."

As the injury situation eased towards the end of the year, it was no accident that this coincided with an upturn in form. Who had been the greatest miss during this period? Certainly the loss of the captain, Brown, was significant, but the Irishman wouldn't single anyone out.

"They were all important to me in various ways but Scott coming back gave the squad a big boost and he was playing very well when he did come back. But they are all important to me in one aspect or another, so it would be unfair to say that one person meant so much to the team as they all played their part."

Fortune certainly hadn't favoured Neil Lennon in the early part of the season but he wasn't ready to concede anything. He had faith in his players' ability to turn things around. Time was of the essence, however. There could be no more slip-ups.

Turning Point

THE shrill of the half-time whistle pierced the air like a signal of distress. Amid a cacophony of jeers, Neil Lennon turned towards the Rugby Park tunnel and headed for the away dressing room. It was a short walk but he had much to ponder. Among the many thoughts which raced across his mind, one burning question loomed large – was he the right man to manage Celtic Football Club? A man of conviction, with confidence in his own ability, he had never entertained these notions of self-doubt before. This was different, though. He was staring into the abyss.

The electronic boards at either end of the ground highlighted the disaster which was unfolding. The scoreline was KILMARNOCK 3-0 CELTIC. It had been a calamitous opening 45 minutes. There was no other way to describe it. A stuttering season was now in danger of complete collapse. As the Irishman opened the door of the dressing room, he knew this would be the most important team-talk of his life.

"I wasn't low. I was angry, I was disappointed. I was questioning myself, because it wasn't acceptable, not for the club, not for the fans but more importantly, not for me," he said. "And I just thought to myself: 'If this is the best you can do with this group of players, then you might have to let someone else come in and pick it up.'

"Another defeat in the manner in which we were playing would have been difficult for me to take. How many points were we behind at the time – ten points? I was looking for a reaction so I went into the dressing room and spoke calmly to them."

His message had the desired effect. He got a response. By full-time, the self-doubt had been set aside. Neil Lennon would fight on – and so would Celtic. The pressure had been building steadily before the trip to Ayrshire. In their previous league outing, Celtic had slumped to a 2-0 defeat to Hearts at Tynecastle. This was a disappointing outcome under normal circumstances but, more significantly, the failure to land another three points had allowed Rangers to extend their advantage at the SPL summit to an eye-watering ten points.

Of the fourteen matches the Hoops had contested during the campaign, they had emerged victorious in just half of them. There had been some standout performances and results but overall, consistency had been lacking. Confidence had gradually ebbed away as a result. While the Hoops retained one game in hand over their city rivals, there was a realisation that the patchy form had to end. The championship dream was fading fast.

"I think there was a real determination amongst us all, the backroom staff and particularly the players to get a consistent run of wins going," said the manager. "We needed to work very hard and get some steel about us to make sure there was a determination to win each and every game. If we didn't play well we still had to make sure we won them, but what we were looking for was the performance as well as the result.

"I had complete faith in the players. They hadn't really hit a vein of form. They had shown it in patches against Motherwell and Dundee United. However, we hadn't put the full package together for a sustained period of time, but I had no doubt that they would."

There had been an enforced break from action following the Tynecastle reversal for another batch of international fixtures. On one hand, the timing was regrettable, removing a swift chance of redemption. Then again, it did present extra time for a number of players to recover from injuries, a frequent inconvenience around this time. Beram Kayal, Cha Du-Ri and Joe Ledley, three important first-team players, all returned from the treatment table in time for the game at Rugby Park. For the rest, there was an opportunity to recharge the batteries for future challenges.

"After a defeat you always want a game as quickly as possible but it just gave the injured players more time to recover," said the Irishman. "It also gave the rest of the guys a chance to get a break, and they came back in looking quite fresh at the start of the week. We had to put away the despondency and disappointment. We had a break where the players could re-energise themselves and have a think about their own game and how they could improve, so they could come back on Thursday and Friday and be really at it, and have a good run between then and Christmas."

The extra preparation time also afforded the manager an opportunity to focus training on areas where standards had fallen short. There was a concerted effort in improving the performance in front of goal.

"We needed to work on that as our play against Hearts was pretty good until the final third and we let ourselves down in that department," added the Irishman. "So we were basically working on that as we only had a small group anyway and there's not a lot of tactical stuff you can do in between.

"We missed good chances at Hearts and as the game went on, at 0-0, they were still in it but we could've come in comfortably one or two ahead at half-time and that would have changed the psychology of what they were trying to do. So we needed to change that mindset in terms of putting teams away when we were in the ascendancy."

Certainly, the expectation was that there would be an emphasis on attack against Kilmarnock, whose manager, Kenny Shiels, had continued to cultivate the same principles employed by his predecessor, Mixu Paatelainen. Despite the departure of some crucial cogs in their team from the previous term, he had successfully scoured the lower leagues in England and elsewhere for suitable replacements to fit into the same attacking mould.

Although their early performances had earned more plaudits than points, there was a growing confidence at Kilmarnock, who had only lost one game at home. They couldn't be afforded space and time to impose their adventurous game-plan.

"Kilmarnock are a good footballing team and they had carried that on from the previous season," said the manager. "They had some decent results early on, even though there had been a few changes. They lost some quality players in Bryson and Eremenko but Kenny Shiels replaced them with his own players. I thought it would be an open, good game of football."

With that in mind, despite the previous indifferent form, Neil Lennon travelled to Kilmarnock confident his players were well-equipped to deliver a much-needed three points. Little did he realise it would be one of the most important ninety minutes of his managerial career so far.

INITIALLY, everything seemed to be going according to plan. Celtic were the better team in the opening stages and fashioned a gilt-edged chance to take the lead in the 12th minute. James Forrest sent Cha scampering clear down the right and the South Korean's cut-back arrived invitingly at the back post for Anthony Stokes. With the goal at his mercy, though, he blazed over.

"We had good control of the game and missed a really good chance early on," reflected the manager. "Cha has made a great run and James has put a great ball through for him. There was a great cross and Anthony was unlucky. It was a great move and would have been a perfect ending to things we had been working on in training all week."

Had it found the net, events may have taken a drastically different course. Instead, Kilmarnock, perhaps buoyed by that miss, started to threaten and took the lead in the 26th minute. Paul Heffernan's chip picked out Dean Shiels, who beat Fraser Forster. That was disappointing, but no-one could have foreseen what was to follow. Celtic's fragile confidence was shaken. Forster was forced into an outstanding save by Liam Kelly's drive from distance. Then in the 39th minute, the hosts added a second. This time the roles were reversed as Shiels supplied Heffernan in the box, and the striker turned the ball home.

Amazingly, on the stroke of half-time, Celtic conceded another goal. Charlie Mulgrew's pass-back was too short, allowing James Fowler to steal in and lob the ball over a helpless Forster into the net. The Celtic support were stunned. It had been a hellish twenty minutes' viewing. Defensively, Celtic had been brittle. All three Kilmarnock goals had been scored with ease. It was hard to fathom how such a sturdy defence in the previous term had descended into such a state of delicacy.

"There didn't seem to be much in the game but we conceded three goals in twenty minutes which was totally unacceptable. We had to do a lot better in stopping crosses and being more urgent and alert at the back, and just being a bit more resolute," said the Irishman. "We had a great chance to go 1-0 up and missed that. But the goals we conceded from our point of view – long balls over the top which we hadn't dealt with properly – was something we had to eradicate very quickly.

"We knew Kilmarnock would play. But then we conceded so many easy goals. Our defensive discipline was poor and we started chasing the game. We were the best defence in the league last year. We had three internationalists in the back four but for some reason there was a nervousness about them. We lost our shape in midfield and we were impotent up front for 20-25 minutes and we had to regroup at half-time. I was as angry as I could possibly be. Defensively we were very poor, in midfield we were poor and the two front boys were poor. As a collective performance it was nowhere near acceptable."

Defeat looked inevitable, which could potentially have left Celtic thirteen points behind Rangers, with the Ibrox side expected to beat St Mirren later that afternoon. Neil Lennon knew his team were better than this. Furious and frustrated, he knew the players had let him, the fans and the club down in the first half. Many managers would have launched a verbal volley at their charges in such circumstances, or hurled the tea cups around the dressing room. It must have been tempting. The Irishman elected to take a different approach, though.

He spoke calmly but forcefully about their wrongs and how to right them. He also elected to make two changes, sending on Mo Bangura and Victor Wanyama for Gary Hooper and Beram Kayal. There was nothing more he could do. It was now up to those on the pitch. The next forty-five minutes would decide his fate. Understanding the gravity of the situation, the Celtic players emerged from the tunnel for the second half. Much to their astonishment, despite the events of the opening period, they were cheered on to the pitch by supporters. They still had faith. And that belief transferred to those on the field.

Battered and bruised, the players had to haul themselves off the canvas and fight for their manager and the fans to save their season.

This wasn't a time for fluency and verve but resolve, fortitude and determination. Gradually, they began to win the battles across the pitch and gain the ascendancy. For a while, it seemed it would be in vain as the home side managed to repel Celtic's attacking advances. However, the Hoops were rewarded for their efforts in the 73rd minute as they finally pulled a goal back. Forrest was fouled twenty-five yards from goal and Stokes atoned for his earlier miss by curling a terrific free-kick into the top corner. It was no more than a glimmer of hope.

Just two minutes later, the deficit was reduced to one. Collecting possession on the edge of the box, Stokes spun and then rifled a shot into the bottom corner. There was real belief now. All the momentum was with the Hoops, and they completed a remarkable comeback three minutes later.

After Forrest had drawn another foul, Ki Sung Yueng launched the resulting free-kick towards the far post. Daniel Majstorovic nodded it across goal and Mulgrew bravely headed home amid a clutch of bodies, sparking scenes of delirium among the travelling fans. In the space of a sensational seven minutes, Celtic had levelled the match. Although they couldn't muster a winner in the closing stages, the draw felt like a victory. In adversity, the Hoops hadn't submitted but shown incredible spirit and desire to salvage a point.

"We asked them at half-time to find the will, belief and the guts to get something out of the game, and they did that," said the manager. "So there were mixed emotions – anger but then I was very proud of the performance in the second half. We had to make the changes for the better of the team and we got the performance in the second half we were looking for.

"Once we got the goal, we always believed we could come back. The players believed it as well. I was very proud of the second half but disgusted with the first. I was angry and proud of them at the same time. Our defending was abysmal in the first half."

The significance of the result was underlined later in the afternoon as St Mirren struck a late leveller to earn a draw with Rangers. A potentially fatal blow to Celtic's title aspirations, which seemed inevitable, had been averted. The gap remained at ten points – substantial yet attainable. It had taken a Herculean effort to rescue some reward from Rugby Park. For forty-five minutes, Celtic had shown they possessed courage and character. Nevertheless, unless it was repeated on a consistent basis, ultimately, it would prove worthless. The dramatic events in Ayrshire had been indicative of the Hoops' Jekyll and Hyde season. It had to halt.

"We hadn't lost ground on the leaders and the players had to take a lot from the second-half performance," said the Irishman. "But we had to start finding consistencies in our performances and find ways of winning games on a regular basis as our form has been pretty patchy.

"I think in a couple of games – Motherwell, Dundee United and some other occasions – over the ninety minutes I had been happy with the performance. There had been spells where we were very good and in other games we hadn't – we had been very disjointed. We said to the players we couldn't afford to keep dropping points because Rangers had been very consistent so far.

"I wanted the players to use the second half to their advantage. Winning football games is hard and winning championships are very difficult things to do. You have to go through hard times in games and some rough patches, where you feel tired but have to find a little bit more. They were out on their feet at the end of the game and I thanked them for their efforts but I was also quite critical of them as it was too inconsistent."

That wasn't just a collective concern. Individually, too many members of the team were not hitting top form regularly enough. Again, this had been showcased at Rugby Park.

"If you take Anthony Stokes as an example," added the manager.

"Overall, I was really pleased with his performance but there were other areas in his game which he could tidy up – simple things. He came out and for twenty minutes he was unplayable against Kilmarnock. He showed me he could do that and I wanted him to do that on a more regular basis.

"We were missing something, whether it was a mindset or a lack of quality in some areas, but that was something we had to improve on. They showed the previous season in abundance that they had it and they showed in the second half at Rugby Park that they had it. So they had to take the performance from the second half and hold on to that for the next four or five months."

There was one player who rightfully earned universal acclaim from the match – James Forrest. From start to finish, the Youth Academy graduate was quite simply magnificent. Belying his tender years and lack of experience he almost single-handedly inspired Celtic's second-half fight-back. Notably, his purposeful attacking forays won free-kicks which led to two of the goals. Overall, his contribution was colossal. Dynamic, determined and skilful, it was a complete performance.

"For me, the king of the day was James Forrest," said the Hoops boss. "I thought he was magnificent from start to finish. It was an immense performance. The kid plays the game that everyone wants to see. He drives the game for you, commits people and is a menace either side. He took the game by the scruff of the neck and dragged the team back into it. For a player of that age, it's to his eternal credit. I had known him for two years but that was the most complete performance I had seen from him since I've known him.

"He's hugely influential in the way we like to play as he has that dynamism and pace, he gets beyond players and stretches teams. But not only that, technically he's very good and has an eye for goal. Already, he had emerged as a very important player, and for one so young, it was excellent progress."

ABOVE all, the Kilmarnock comeback was a personal triumph for Neil Lennon. At the point where the pressure had been at its most intense, when it seemed there was no way back, he met the challenge and came out the other side. His intervention at the break roused Celtic from their slumber. It was a huge test of his managerial abilities and one which he passed with distinction.

"I said to myself, 'Right, this is your biggest test yet, let's see what you can do and see if you can get the response from the players that you're looking for,'" he said. "Thankfully we did. It was nothing to do with being great at tactics or anything like that. It was about pushing the players to dig deep and get something out of the game. You have to do your job, motivate your players and motivate yourself. We made a couple of switches, which we felt we needed to."

Although the players had failed to achieve expected standards in the first half, the manager knew that he bore ultimate responsibility. This was his team. He had carefully constructed and nurtured it for nearly eighteen months. It had almost crumbled in front of his eyes. That was hard to take. Another horror show in the second half would have been too much to bear. It could have been the end.

"Another defeat in the manner of which we were playing would have been difficult for me to take. When we lost three soft goals at Kilmarnock I began to think, 'Is this a reflection on me? Is this my team here?' I was asking myself those questions and when we were 3-0 down I thought, 'Do I hand in my resignation after the game if it goes to four or five?'

"That scoreline would've been totally unacceptable for someone like me, even though I'd never been put under any pressure from upstairs. I didn't think we were in such a bad position that the sack was looming, but if the gap between us Rangers had widened then I could have understood if the sack had been mentioned. The one thing I didn't do was hit the panic button and when you come out the other side of something like that you think, 'Do you know what? You did all right there and you can do it again.'"

Exactly what the Irishman said to players in the Rugby Park dressing room that day will never be fully revealed. By general rule, what is uttered within those four walls stays there. However, it altered the course of Celtic's season. Even at the time, it felt like a turning point. The mixed early-season form had plumbed new depths during that disastrous first forty-five. Celtic appeared in an irreversible slide until the manager's intervention at the break. A line in the sand had been drawn. Resolve, team spirit and togetherness had came to the fore in the second half and would remain in evidence throughout the rest of the season. In deepest adversity, Celtic didn't break, they drew strength. The 3-3 draw at Kilmarnock would be the first match in a remarkable 26-game domestic unbeaten run. It was the springboard. Although they actually fell further behind Rangers in the title race over the next few weeks, mainly as a result of fixture scheduling, the lead was gradually chipped away until it was completely eroded.

"I wanted a positive reaction and I got it," said the manager. "It spoke volumes for the players that they showed great character and quality, particularly in the final 20 minutes – resilience, belief. I wouldn't say it was a trigger point for what was to come but it was certainly a foundation for it. I always believed in the players that they could turn it around. They did that."

Fifteen
To Won

AMID the turbulence created by Celtic's erratic early-season form, Neil Lennon remained resolute. He was convinced the players at his disposal were capable of delivering success. His style of management never altered. He held his nerve and was richly rewarded as Celtic embarked on a remarkable twenty-match winning run in domestic football.

The revival was never the result of revolution or one momentous happening. It was a gradual process based on hard work, fortitude and belief. Celtic had lacked confidence and consistency. Both slowly returned as matches were won, creating an unstoppable force.

"Football is unpredictable and nothing surprises me," said the manager. "I always believed in the team and felt we would find our consistency, but I worried that it would be too late. But we found it and put a fantastic run together of seventeen or eighteen wins and that is special at any level of football. It just built and built and the confidence oozed. Now these are all words I am coming out with now. At the time it was still a very difficult thing to do.

"People look on it as a matter of fact. It's not. The players had to really focus, look after themselves and sacrifice a lot of things to get back in the championship run and it culminated in beating Rangers in December. We turned around a huge deficit in a short space of time."

The stirring second-half comeback at Kilmarnock was the spark, but it didn't instigate an immediate upturn in fortunes. That took time. Celtic earned two more draws, along with three wins in the aftermath of Rugby Park. The run of losses had been halted yet the flames of recovery would only be fanned through a sustained series of victories. The starting point arrived at Fir Park in early November. Celtic went into the game in third place behind their opponents and Rangers, who held a fifteen-point advantage at the SPL summit. Although they still held two games in reserve over the Ibrox side, the pressure remained firmly on Neil Lennon's shoulders. And he was tired of having to explain the reasons for failure. It was time to kick into gear.

"I thought we were gradually getting better but you were always wary that the lack of consistency would let you down," he said. "I was fed up of having to say it to the supporters and I was fed up of having these team-talks with the players afterwards – we had to start winning games on a consistent basis. Even if that meant scratching out a 1-0 win, we had to find a way of doing it. We had the players who were capable of doing that but they weren't playing as consistently as I would have liked them to. That was my job and maybe I was not doing something right, but it was hard to put my finger on it."

That said, Celtic had been handed a timely boost days ahead of the game courtesy of a 3-1 triumph over Rennes in the Europa League. The French side made the breakthrough in the opening five minutes but an Anthony Stokes double and a Gary Hooper strike completed an impressive comeback for an injury-hit Celtic side, who were forced to field 17-year-old Marcus Fraser for the second half.

However, Celtic had been developing a worrying habit of conceding early goals, a failing highlighted once more against Motherwell as Michael Higdon headed home in the 11th minute. Then again, the Hoops had also harnessed a greater resilience on the back of the Kilmarnock fightback and swiftly restored parity through Anthony Stokes' volley. The rest of the game was a fierce battle, with both sides enjoying periods of pressure. But it was the introduction of Paddy McCourt and Hooper from the bench which turned the game in Celtic's favour.

In typical fashion, the mercurial Irishman skipped past several challenges from deep inside his own half before finding Stokes in the box. The striker's driven cross was duly turned home by Hooper. It was a must-win match – and Celtic delivered. They leapfrogged Motherwell into second place and reduced the gap with Rangers to twelve points. A big hurdle had been overcome, but many more lay ahead.

"I was really pleased with the win at Motherwell," said the manager. "Under real pressure and going a goal down, we got the equaliser and I thought in the second half we were very good. Considering that Motherwell were ahead of us going into the game, we needed to win it. We showed a bit of character again after losing the early goal. It was poor from us.

"But the response was great. We scored a great goal from a corner, Sammi got a great touch on it and Stokesy has peeled away and finished brilliantly. After that we settled into the game quite well and I thought in the second half we played very well. We were very strong, we looked fit and we finished the game really strongly as well and we thoroughly deserved to win, particularly on chances made.

"There was a good defensive display. I don't remember Fraser having a lot to do in the game. There was a real will to win. Stokesy led the line really well, the two boys in midfield worked very hard and the back-four were excellent. They did a really good job on their attacking players. I thought Sammi put in another good shift for us and then the two subs came on and won us the game. I was delighted by their contributions as well."

In contrast to the previous international breaks, Celtic had entered the latest one on a high and with fresh impetus. The gap in competitive duty also allowed further time to clear an increasingly busy treatment table. The gloom was beginning to clear – but no one could have predicted what was about to follow.

"There was a long way to go in the season," the Hoops boss said. "Things were starting to look a bit brighter. We had lost one in eleven or twelve games, and I know there had been a couple of draws in there but the team were starting to really gel again and find their feet."

Now the key was building momentum. Celtic hadn't won three successive games since the opening three weeks of the season. Standing in their way to repeating that feat was Inverness Caley Thistle. Terry Butcher's side had recently routed Kilmarnock 6-3 on their travels, and given Celtic traditionally found the going difficult in the Highlands, it was another formidable obstacle to negotiate. An injury-depleted squad headed north determined to build on the win at Fir Park.

"We had watched them and had done a bit of analysis of their previous match against Kilmarnock and they were fantastic," said the manager. "They were full of energy, full of quality and they could have scored more than six. Bearing in mind they were playing at home as well, it was going to be a tough proposition for us and we had to be at our best. It was an early kick-off and some of our players had been away on international duty, so we had to work very hard on them."

The first-half dismissal of Caly midfielder, Greg Tansey, after he clashed with Georgios Samaras in an aerial tussle, handed the Hoops the ascendancy. Celtic capitalised on their numerical advantage after the break as Stokes bagged a brace to seal a 2-0 win.

"We were given an extra man away from home and that gave us a psychological lift," said the Hoops boss. "We were solid and were creating chances even when it was 11 v 11. I was upset we weren't ahead by the time Inverness went down to ten men but that was the only thing that annoyed me. It's always difficult there and the pitch was poor. The grass was long and it made it bumpy so we weren't able to play slick, quick football. We wanted our players to adapt to the conditions first and play accordingly.

"The shape of the team was good and the application was excellent. The game opened up for us in the second half and the two goals were well worked. It was important to keep the winning run going after the break. We were starting to get consistency from individual players that hadn't been there before, and the other players who had been playing well in the season were continuing in the same vein."

The on-form Stokes was now on eleven goals for the season. He had scored five goals in three games, helping to propel the Bhoys to three wins on the spin.

"He was playing very well and what pleased me more was that his all-round game was improving," added the Irishman. "He was a huge player in those couple of months."

Back in Glasgow, Rangers could only draw with St Johnstone. The gap was now down to ten points and it would be diminished further if Celtic could extract maximum reward from their game in hand against Dunfermline. With that carrot, Celtic began the game with gusto and purpose in Paradise, opening up a two-goal lead by the quarter-hour mark. Hooper took advantage of a poor defensive pass to break the deadlock, before Forrest swept home a rebound after Stokes' shot had been saved. When the winger won a penalty in the second half, the points appeared safe. However, Ki Sung Yueng missed from the spot and Andy Barrowman's late consolation caused a few late flutters.

In spite of Celtic's rapid start and dominance, it was relief which greeted the final whistle. Still, it was job done. There were now just seven points separating the Hoops from the SPL summit. That was important. But the manager was more concerned about preserving the winning form as Celtic prepared for their next fixture against St Mirren. The foot had to remain firmly on the gas.

"I wasn't really considering cutting the gap or anything like that – it was basically about keeping this winning run going," he said. "We were at home and wanted to maximise home advantage in our favour. Some players were coming back to the form we knew they were capable of. Four wins in a row was good consistency but at a club like this where the expectations are high, the demands are great on the players – but they knew that. We had played some brilliant football against Dunfermline and I was thrilled with that. It was the best we had played at home for a while, and I just hoped we could continue in the same vein."

Those on the field answered his call. Fuelled with renewed belief from their recent success, Celtic blitzed the Buddies, racking up their biggest winning margin of the season. The final score was 5-0 to the hosts. Arguably it had been the best home showing of the season. Samaras opened the scoring, before Hooper highlighted his return to form with a terrific hat-trick. Dylan McGeouch capped off a perfect day with a contender for goal of the season on his home bow. Winning possession deep in Celtic territory, the teenager surged forward, evaded several challenges and drilled a shot into the corner. Cue bedlam. The rain was torrential at Celtic Park but the gloom had lifted. Rangers slumped to defeat at Kilmarnock. Five consecutive wins, five goals – the gap was just four.

"We just seemed to be hitting form," said the manager. "It had been coming for a while. It was very pleasing. When we played liked that, it was a joy to watch. We'd got off to a good start, which always helps. We did the same against Dunfermline, creating a lot of good chances and I felt we were more clinical against St Mirren, who I felt were a better team as well.

"We were strong throughout the group and the attacking play was of a very high standard. I thought our back four were great. They held a good line and the two centre-halves looked like they dovetailed quite well. Joe Ledley and Adam Matthews on either flank gave us so much energy defensively and offensively. The two boys in midfield were tremendous – really strong, aggressive in the tackle and they read the game well. They kept us ticking over. The four boys going forward were all on top form, and I just thought Gary Hooper was brilliant. His link-up play was excellent. He looked really strong and healthy."

Rangers' lead had been whittled down to four points in under a month. It was a remarkable achievement. Celtic were back in the race. Nonetheless, this was just the start. Now they had the Ibrox side in their sights, the aim had to be to draw level and be in a position to overtake.

"I felt if we got some consistency into our game we would start clawing the lead back," said the Irishman. "We had done it and were almost within touching distance. We still had a lot of work ahead of us and there was still a lot of football to be played this season. But the momentum was with us and we just had to maintain that."

THE buoyancy was back. No doubt about it. Not even a narrow defeat to Atletico Madrid in the Europa League could knock Celtic off their stride. A spirited showing against the La Liga side deserved some tangible recompense rather than plaudits. The European reversal had ended the winning sequence in all competitions but the domestic run remained intact, and Neil Lennon was anxious to preserve it as Celtic prepared for the tricky league clash at Dundee United.

"It was a priority," he said. "Tannadice is always a great ground to go and play in, and Dundee United had had a good result the previous weekend, going to Fir Park and getting a point."

Celtic made a bright start and deservedly went in front in the 12th minute through Gary Hooper. Collecting a pass from James Forrest, the striker confidently smashed a low shot into the net. It was enough to collect the full points. Although Celtic lacked attacking inspiration for the remainder of the contest, they comfortably dealt with any of the home side's forward flurries. Despite the small margin of advantage, the destination of the points was never in question. As the winter weather slowed down much of the country, Celtic's forward momentum showed no sign of abating.

"I was thrilled with the three points," said the manager. "It kept the run going and credit to the players for going there and winning. I was delighted. It was a great three points for us, a clean sheet, and we had some really good performances. I thought the first half was as good as we had played away from home this season in terms of pace and intensity. We pressed them really well and scored a good goal. I think the early goal gave us a huge lift, and it was a great goal.

"Going forward we were very good and could have been a couple up. You always need that second goal, though, and I just felt in the second half we weren't as productive in the final third as we could've been and that was the difference in us not winning the game more comfortably. To be fair, I never really saw Fraser in any real trouble, particularly in the first half where I thought we were in total control of the game."

There was more good news for the Bhoys as captain, Scott Brown, penned a contract extension until 2015, with the option of a further year. He was also given another outing as a second-half substitute against United as he continued his recovery from long-term injury.

"It was tremendous news that Scott signed his contract," said the manager. "He was always committed to the club. I knew that, and I was absolutely delighted it had been sorted out."

Celtic's resurgence was reflected in the SPL's monthly prize-giving for November as the club swept the board – Neil Lennon was awarded Manager of the Month, Gary Hooper, Player of the Month and James Forrest, Young Player of the Month.

"It was a tribute to the players, more than myself or the individual awards that Gary and James won, although those two were outstand-ing," said the Hoops boss. "The confidence was back in the players, the consistency was back, and it was a big month in terms of winning games and clawing back the gap. I was very pleased with the charac-ter the team had shown under pressure at times. I just think the atti-tude and application, the bit of quality which was maybe lacking, the work-rate and the tempo of the games had got a lot better, along with players finding their form."

Receiving recognition is always a welcome fillip but the league silver was the only target in Celtic's crosshair. The next focus was on beat-ing Hearts – the last team to have inflicted defeat on the Hoops – in their next fixture and chalk up win number six. Despite the Tynecastle side's off-field struggles at that juncture, which had dominated the back pages during the build-up, this was a game laced with potential pitfalls.

"It could have spurred them on as a motivation – they could've been like a wounded animal in that respect," said the Irishman. "But we approached the game like we approached every other game, regardless of the opposition. Hearts had been a wee bit inconsistent with their results, but we knew on their day they could be a very dangerous team. As regards our own situation, we had had five consecutive wins and it was important we kept that run going."

The visitors attempted to frustrate Celtic, erecting a defensive barrier which the Hoops, although dominating possession, found difficult to penetrate. It took a moment of magic to break the deadlock. With eighteen minutes remaining, Victor Wanyama fastened on to a bouncing ball and fizzed a ferocious shot into the top corner from twenty-five yards.

But Celtic had Fraser Forster to thank for earning maximum reward. In the final minute, after Wanyama had been harshly penalised for handball, the keeper sprang to his left and pushed away Eggert Jonsson's penalty. It was a dramatic finale to an absorbing and nervy contest. The Hoops had persevered and seen it through. That took a strong mentality.

"The fact is, the players believed in themselves and kept playing and, but for a bit of luck, we could have won the game a bit more comfortably," said the manager. "To be fair to Hearts that's the best they had played here for a while in terms of their team shape and their morale. It's always a dangerous game when adverse circumstances bring out the best out in a team. So I think they showed a lot of team spirit. There was a great solidarity among our team. You saw the reaction after Fraser saved the penalty and when Victor scored the goal. The spirit was fantastic. It was a very buoyant dressing room afterwards."

This was an important asset over the hectic festive fixture period. A 1-1 draw in Italy against Udinese saw Celtic bow out of Europe with their heads held high. They required a win to progress from a tough group and were unfortunate not do so following a courageous display. On their return to domestic duties, Celtic remained on their travels for the shorter journey to Perth, where they faced St Johnstone. Like Hearts, this was another team who had beaten Celtic earlier in the campaign. Indeed, it was the Saints who had halted the Hoops' one hundred per cent start to the campaign. A crucial confidence-breaker.

This time Celtic would not be denied as they made it a magnificent seven wins on the spin. The first half was devoid of goals but on the hour mark Hooper bundled home from a corner to reward the domi-nant visitors. Ki Sung Yueng got the decisive touch to a wonderful counter-attack to bag the points four minutes later.

"We had played very well against a top-class team in Udinese and the question was, could we repeat that consistently? Well we did that against St Johnstone," said the manager. "There were some brilliant individual performances and as a team we were excellent. It was prob-ably as good as we had played away from home all season, particularly off the back of a European game. I thought from start to finish we were right at it and the score could have been a lot higher.

"You're always worried at 0-0, especially coming in at half-time, so we asked the players for a little bit more in the final third. We had good control of the game, physically we were strong and our back four were excellent. The second goal was one of our goals of the season – it was a brilliant team goal. James Forrest picked out Ki, but Sammi did well to pick Jamesy out. He could have shot but he had the presence of mind to pick out Ki who had made a seventy-yard run. He then showed great composure to finish it off and I was thrilled with the goal."

Another measure of revenge was in the air on Christmas Eve as Celtic took on Kilmarnock. Less than two months previously, half-time at Rugby Park in October had been the nadir of the season – three goals down and in danger of becoming detached from the leading pack. Quite a turnaround. Four days later the second Glasgow derby of the season would be contested. This wasn't the time to falter.

"Seven wins in a row was good form but it could go at any time and we had to be wary of that. The St Johnstone win was important because Rangers had won the day before and we wanted to keep our run going. We did that and there was a very positive feeling going into the game against Kilmarnock. They had taken two points off us at Rugby Park so again it was a game we had to be wary of."

News of Rangers' defeat against St Mirren in the early kick-off amplified the incentive. A victory for Celtic would cut the lead to a solitary point before the visit of Rangers, and Samaras helped achieve that feat, bagging a double with goals either side of half-time. The Hoops survived a few late nervy moments, but held on to claim a 2-1 triumph. Rangers were now within touching distance.

Confidence was naturally brimming on the back of eight successive wins. This was an enormous asset ahead of such an important game. The only potential fall-out in such circumstances was self-satisfaction. Nonetheless, this was remote and steps had been taken to contain any breakout.

"Momentum is important, as long as you don't take complacency into the game, and I was sure the players wouldn't do that because they knew what was at stake," said the Hoops boss. "We knew if we won the game we would go top of the table, and our focus was on winning the game. If that was the reward of it, so be it. We just wanted to make our home advantage count and keep the winning run going. It was very important to the players – they were in a good vein of form – but we were playing our biggest rivals."

Having trailed the Ibrox side by fifteen points before the Motherwell match, Celtic were in a position to start the New Year as championship leaders. It had been an astonishing turnaround.

"I always believed we would close the gap, but I didn't realise we would do it so quickly," he said. "But that was testament to the players' consistency and the fact that they went on this winning run. There was a huge amount of football still to be played over the next four or five months. We had just been looking at one game at a time and trying to eat into the lead, and we had done that."

The match was a typical Glasgow derby – frenetic, furious and fiercely-fought. It was decided by one goal, and it went to Celtic. After a goal-less first half, the Hoops stormed forward with intent at the restart and were rewarded as Joe Ledley headed powerfully past Allan McGregor from a corner. It was a lead they never looked in danger of relinquishing. The final whistle sparked scenes of jubilation. Celtic had completed a turnaround which scarcely seemed possible.

"I was so proud of the players and I thought it was, without being brilliant, a very good performance against a dogged Rangers side," said the manager. "It was always going to take the first goal to settle either team and thankfully we got it. Nine wins in a row is no mean feat. It was the best run domestically since I had taken charge, and we just wanted to go again. There was a lot of football to be played but this gave the players a lot of confidence, as long as they didn't get complacent. It was for the fans more than anything else, because it gave our supporters a sense of pride going into the New Year."

CELTIC had closed the gap, drew level and then overtaken Rangers. The challenge now was to stamp their authority in the title race by extending the points advantage. Neil Lennon knew the key was to maintain their forward momentum – to keep winning. The Hoops need not look elsewhere anymore. The chasing pack was behind them. Their destiny was within their own hands. All they had to do was focus on each game in turn, and continue to earn maximum points. By doing that, there would be no challenge to their supremacy.

The first fixture following the win over Rangers was an away fixture at bottom-side Dunfermline. Determined not to let their previous good work go to waste, Celtic were convincing 3-0 victors at East End Park, preserving their two-point lead. Anthony Stokes, Victor Wanyama and Charlie Mulgrew were all on target for the visitors in a match they bossed from start to finish. Emilio Izaguirre's first appearance since his long-term lay-off as a second-half substitute was also a welcome sight.

"It's a great feeling to win a derby game," said the manager. "But you are always wary of the fall-out and hangover of it. You're on a high and there is a bit of a comedown, but it was a great away win, a clean sheet and some great goals and a very good performance. I was delighted.

"I thought the attitude was spot-on and the application, work-rate and team spirit were fantastic. You need that when you're away from home, no matter who you are playing. Dunfermline had made it very difficult for us to break them down. It took a great individual goal to get us going but I thought we controlled ninety per cent of the game. I couldn't speak highly enough of the efforts of the players."

There was a comfortable passage past Third Division Peterhead in the Scottish Cup fourth-round before Celtic hosted Dundee United in the SPL. Rangers had won earlier in the day, meaning the Hoops started the game in second place. Two goals in the opening quarter signalled their intent to return to top spot. Gary Hooper drilled home after being supplied by Stokes. Five minutes later, Victor Wanyama, December's SPL Player of the Month, slammed a header in from a corner. The visitors, who were beginning to show signs of resurgence, reduced the deficit through John Rankin's drive from distance. However, Celtic held firm to move back into first position and seal win number twelve.

"It was a good performance against a team that played very well against us, particularly in the second half," said the Hoops boss. "I thought in the first half we were excellent, played some really good football and scored two very good goals. It could have been more, and then we started the second half again very well and made the goal-keeper work a couple of times.

"Then, out of the blue, Dundee United scored a really great goal themselves, and that can happen in football. The psychology of the game changes a little bit. Dundee United got a lift from that and we needed Fraser to make a good save from Jon Daly. But I thought we finished the game well, and Sammi had a couple of great chances to kill the game off. Unfortunately, he didn't take them, but overall I was delighted by it. At times in the game we probably didn't compete as well as we should have done, or pass the ball as well as we could have, but I wasn't going to be overly critical of the players because of the form they had shown."

It was a rare reversal of roles for Celtic the following week as they were afforded the opportunity to play before Rangers and exert extra pressure on their city rivals. A win for Celtic would stretch their lead to five points before kick-off at Ibrox. It was a chance the manager was keen to exploit.

"For me, going into the game, it was an advantage playing first but we had to make the most of that opportunity," he explained. "If we won the game we would be five points clear before they started, so that was a huge motivation for us."

However, the Irishman recognised the scale of the threat posed by St Mirren on their home patch, which was evident by their recent success against Rangers.

"They had beaten Rangers recently so they were capable of beating anyone at home," he added. "But our form against St Mirren over the last couple of years had been good so we wanted to maintain that."

Notwithstanding the swirling winds and driving rain, this was one of the toughest examinations Celtic faced all season. Fraser Forster came to the Hoops' rescue on several occasions as the hosts pressed for the vital breakthrough.

But the visitors, displaying admirable resilience and will-to-win, fought on and, helped by the introduction of Anthony Stokes and Kris Commons from the bench, gained the ascendancy as the match neared its conclusion. With twenty minutes left, James Forrest fired a controlled effort into the corner and as the final whistle approached, Scott Brown's curling effort from eighteen yards nestled in the top corner. Celtic had stood firm. Later in the day, Rangers were unable to beat Aberdeen at Ibrox. The Hoops were four points clear. Win number thirteen had been hard-earned – and significant.

"It was the toughest game we had experienced so far in the run, against a really good St Mirren team, in atrocious conditions," reflected the manager. "I needed my goalkeeper to make some great saves and he did, but I thought we created plenty of good chances. You're not always going to play scintillating football and there are times you are going to have to show great character and resolve.

"They threw the kitchen sink at us second half but we saw it off and scored two very good goals – Jamesy got the breakthrough and Scott scored a great second goal. Defensively we were excellent and Fraser had a great day. It was a big, big win for us, huge in the context of the season. We expected to be put under pressure and we said we would wait until the last minute, like we did last year, but thankfully it came a little bit earlier this year. In the majority of games this season, once they got that breakthrough they were able to go on and win the games. They were able to see the games out and usually get another one. In a lot of these games the first goal is very important."

Celtic switched competitions for the next two weeks – but there was the same end result. In the Scottish Communities League Cup semi-final, a plucky Falkirk were dispatched 3-1 at Hampden, before the Hoops safely negotiated the test of Inverness Caley Thistle in the Scottish Cup fifth-round. The Celtic juggernaut rolled on. Indeed, it had yet to reach full speed. On the cusp of extending their winning streak to sixteen games, Celtic took on Hearts at Tynecastle, the venue they last tasted defeat. This was a different team to then, though, not in make-up but in confidence and resolve. For the manager it was simply another game, with another three points at stake.

"It was the most important game of the season because it was the next one," he said. "There was no extra significance attached to the fixture because of the previous defeat, though that served as a warning – not that any was needed – that it would be an extremely tough fixture against Hearts. I thought we were in a different place to where we were then. Confidence was good, the team was playing very well, and the players were taking a lot of pride in what they were doing. We had a chance to extend our lead at the top of the table and put the pressure on everybody else."

They did more: they set down a statement of intent. Celtic were imperious in the capital – determined, fluent and ruthless. At times, it was breathtaking to watch. After surviving an early scare when Stephen Elliott's header appeared to cross the line, the Hoops rubbed salt in the wounds when Brown fired home from the resultant break-away. As Celtic zipped the ball around the pitch with poise and purpose, Wanyama and Joe Ledley were also on target before the break. There was little let-up in the second half as the visitors continued to dictate proceedings, much to the joy of a raucous travelling support. Hooper stabbed number four on sixty minutes. Devastating.

"It was just a really powerful performance – the intensity of the game and the pace we played at," reflected the manager. "We were clinical and very professional. We played some really good football and really blew Hearts away that night. Coming off, you know you are coming away with a really good side. It's very difficult to maintain that level of performance every week, I understand that, but the players had shown they could do it.

"It was as good as we had played at Tynecastle. They were just getting better and better. Individual performances and the overall team performance were just magnificent. I believe the ball was over the line so we caught a break there, but the response we got from the team was fantastic. We scored four, going on six or seven, so I'm not sure it had a massive bearing on the game. It might have given Hearts a psychological edge, but there was a long, long way to go in the game from there, and the mood the players were in was great. That's what Celtic teams are all about."

It was the perfect prelude to the manager's 100th game in charge, which came a few days later at Paradise against Inverness Caley Thistle. At that moment he was on a huge high. However, there had been some almighty lows, too. It had been a rollercoaster ride. But he had savoured every minute.

"It didn't seem like one hundred games – it seemed like a lot more," said the Hoops boss. "We had crammed so much in. There had been some great highs and some very bad lows. But that's life at Celtic for you – I'm sure it's life at every major club. I thoroughly enjoy the job and the challenges that always lie ahead. You are never comfortable because you are only ever one adverse result away from a crisis, if you want to call it that, and some things get blown out of proportion. What I had been able to do was to keep a level mood, going through the bad spell, and then we were going through a good spell, just staying on a plain which suits the players and me best."

He was able to celebrate the milestone with a victory courtesy of Joe Ledley's solitary strike. The Welshman had struck early in the first half and the Hoops seemed in charge of affairs. However, the controversial dismissal of Daniel Majstorovic on the hour mark increased the tension. Parity of numbers was restored under twenty minutes later, though, as the visitors' Steve Williams also saw red, and the home side saw out the game with ease thereafter. Two different displays in the space of a week but, ultimately, the same reward.

"It was a tough game and we had to contend with a lot of things, so I was delighted with the win and the clean sheet," said the manager. "I was pleased with the players. They showed great character again, and they came through it with flying colours. In the main we were in the ascendancy until the sending off and then that gave Inverness a lift. But the way the players conducted themselves was very pleasing.

"Things were going very well but we knew there was still a long way to go. I was wary of the game on the back of Wednesday night at Tynecastle but the attitude and quality at times was impressive. It wasn't a vintage performance but it was pretty solid against a very tough Inverness team, who'd had a week's rest and had freshened things up a little bit."

Celtic were four points ahead of Rangers at this stage but found that advantage rocket to fourteen prior to their fixture with Hibernian the next weekend, following the Ibrox side's ten-point deduction for entering administration. The Hoops weren't distracted, though. They were keen to dish out a second helping of capital punishment at Easter Road.

"We couldn't control what went on elsewhere," said the manager. "What we always try and do is take care of our own business as best we can. We were at the forefront of a very good run and our aim was to keep that run going for as long as we possibly could. The players were pretty proud of what they had achieved but they had won nothing yet, and that was their incentive, regardless of what was going on elsewhere."

Celtic went one better than Tynecastle, running Hibs ragged, scoring five unanswered goals. Hooper bagged a brace, Stokes plundered his customary goal at his former hunting ground, while Charlie Mulgrew and Ki were also on target. With Rangers falling to defeat against Kilmarnock the previous day, the Hoops were now seventeen points clear and stretching away into the distance. The party was already underway among the Celtic supporters behind one of the goals at Easter Road.

"Again, it could have been easy to be distracted but we hadn't really talked about what was going on elsewhere," said the manager. "The backslapping could come if and when we got over the line, but there was still a bit of work to do before that. We wanted them to have the right attitude going into the game and the right application, teamwork and work-rate was there for all to see.

"It was a great three points but more importantly, the performance was fantastic. From start to finish we were on the front foot. The two front men set the tone for the rest of the team – I asked them to do that. Their attitude, their work off the ball, their hunger to get the ball back and the quality they showed in the final third were all very pleasing. I was delighted with the way they were playing, I was delighted with their athleticism and conditioning – allied to that, they could play football. They entertained the Celtic fans at Easter Road and everyone associated with the club went home happy."

The Hoops had scored nine goals in their last two away games. The conditions on the road seemed to suit.

"We probably played our most powerful football away from home because teams come at you a bit more and we can pick them off, whereas at times at Celtic Park we have to be a little bit more patient and the game maybe isn't as free-flowing as it could be," added the Irishman.

No-one looked capable of halting the Hoops' charge to the championship, particularly the team propping up the league for most of the season, Dunfermline, who visited Paradise for a midweek fixture. That thought wasn't being entertained by the manager, however.

"It was huge game and we couldn't look back," he said. "The game at Easter Road had gone and Dunfermline were fighting for their lives. They had made life difficult for the last ten minutes at Celtic Park the last time, but if the team's attitude was as good as it was at Easter Road then it would have taken a good team to stop us."

The winning streak was also approaching the record set by the manager's formidable team when he was a player back in 2004.

"They took a lot pride in it," said the Hoops boss. "Runs like this don't come around very often in any season. It was just a question of ticking off the games and winning them, and trying to win them in a bit of style. It's not easy. Winning games is hard but these boys were in a good place at the time."

There would be no upset. Goals in each half from Mulgrew and Forrest confirmed the three points for a dominant Celtic, with Pars keeper, Chris Smith, performing heroics to keep the scoreline respectable.

"I thought we made it hard for ourselves," said the manager. "The only criticism I had of the team was that we were wasteful in front of goal. Apart from that, I was very proud of the team. I was proud of the way they had played. They had kept that winning run going and opened up a huge gap in the championship, so I couldn't ask any more of them really. We could have easily switched off, and they could have gone home, saying we had chucked that one away but they didn't and I was delighted with that."

Celtic had now surged a mammoth twenty points ahead of their rivals. By force of fate, the opportunity of amassing an astonishing twenty wins on the spin came against third-placed Motherwell – the first meeting of the sides since the run of victories first began back in November. The Hoops had never looked back from that moment, storming to the league summit, while the Steelmen, to their credit, had maintained their lofty position.

"We were obviously playing very well and were at home, and we wanted to make this place a difficult venue for people to come," said the manager. "Confidence was running high through both squads. Motherwell were having an exceptional season. I had watched them the previous week against Hearts at Fir Park and they had played some great football, thoroughly deserved to win and could have won by more, and that was even with them down to ten men for forty minutes in the game."

It may not have been a thrilling contest, but it was absorbing, nonetheless. The hosts bossed proceedings, while Motherwell were well-organised and offered stubborn resistance. Eventually Hooper found a way through in the 59th minute, sweeping home from close-range after Samaras had chested the ball into his path. Forster enjoyed a quiet afternoon at the other end as the Steelmen's much-vaunted attack failed to threaten a late leveller. Indeed, it was Celtic who looked the more likely to add to the tally. Although it wasn't the best display of the run, once again, the team's fortitude had been remarkable.

"It wasn't a vintage performance but that was understandable as it had been a hectic week for the players, and that was eight goals in three games and none conceded, so I couldn't ask any more of them really," he said. "I thought we were always on top in the game. Motherwell played very well but I don't think they had any clear-cut chances or any concerted period of pressure.

"We were a bit flat in the first half but going forward in the second half I felt we were a lot better and we scored a good goal. I was so proud of them and wanted them to keep it going as runs like that come once in their career so I didn't want them to take their foot off the pedal."

In an act of symmetry, it proved the final game in the winning run. The following week, Celtic could only manage a 1-1 draw at Pittodrie against an in-form Aberdeen. There were several mitigating factors: chiefly, being denied the services of a number of international players because of the early kick-off in the North East, and losing a goal through a cruel deflection.

Nonetheless, Celtic's season had come full circle during these twenty games. It had been an incredible collective effort by the squad. They had broken records, set by some of the greatest Celtic teams of the past and achieved something which seemed not just remote but almost impossible. The SPL finishing line was in sight and no one else was in the picture. Neil Lennon was immensely proud.

"Under the circumstances I was disappointed that the run was over but it was completely understandable, considering the way the game was scheduled," he said. "I was very disappointed with that because we had no time to get our players back and get them recovered. We scored a good goal and we lost one through a deflection, so I was immensely proud of the players in the way they'd handled things over the previous three or four months. The winning run was over but the unbeaten run continued. The players and supporters were rightly proud of that."

Euro Zone

EUROPE has become a byword for gloom, bleakness and hardship in recent times. The financial crisis engulfing the Euro-zone has cast a dark shadow over the continent, making it synony-mous with bad news. Not for Celtic. Not for Neil Lennon. The club's participation in the Europa League in 2011/12 was a crucial cog in the team's revival and success. Confidence from a series of impressive performances and results in the competition helped propel Celtic to the title. Far from being a distraction to domestic duties – a view some outside of the club had subscribed to – it proved to be an inspiration.

Although the Hoops ended their continental campaign before Christmas, finishing third in a group which included Atletico Madrid, Udinese and Rennes, it was a gallant effort from such a youthful and inexperienced side. Their standard of performance steadily improved in each game as they became more streetwise with their surroundings. By the end, the Hoops were extremely unfortunate not to progress from, arguably, the most demanding section in the entire tournament. It was no coincidence that Celtic's resurgence in the SPL was concurrent to their improving results in Europe. A diversion? Hardly.

"It is a nonsense," said the manager. "Europe is difficult, mentally and physically, but we are a big club and when you want to be a top player these are the demands put upon you, and I would rather be in Europe than not. There were a lot of pivotal games. We did okay in Madrid, where I thought we could have done better. Against Udinese we were excellent but got done by a very dubious penalty decision to draw the game, but it was the two games against Rennes that gave the players a big lift.

"We had a real shadow squad. We had to bring on players like Marcus Fraser, so that really delighted me and it gave the club and the squad a huge boost. Again, we played well against Atletico Madrid, who won the competition not so long ago, so it shows the quality of the team they were. We tried to even up the score in the first half-hour and then they scored a very good goal, but they were a quality side and we expected that.

"All you can ask for is a performance and we got that. I'm always looking for the win but it was small steps at a time. For me, the highlight of it was going to Udinese and playing brilliantly. We had one cleared off the line in the last minute, which would have put us through. But the overall performance, and the fact we didn't just go there to defend but actually came out and attacked Udinese when we could, was pleasing. There was a maturity and intelligence about the performance and an understanding of the awareness in the team, and that really gave them a real boost of confidence for the rest of the season."

Making a greater impression on Europe was one of the Irishman's prime objectives ahead of the season. There were patent financial rewards for an extended continental campaign, yet that was just one of many incentives for the manager. Prestige, player development and the prevailing pain from exiting at the first hurdle in the previous campaign were all motivating factors.

Celtic's entrance to the group section was, of course, rather unusual. Drawn against FC Sion in the play-off qualifier, the Hoops lost 3-1 on aggregate. However, the Swiss side had flouted a transfer ban, selecting several ineligible players in both legs and were subsequently thrown out the competition by UEFA. With all the court cases, appeals and bullish statements initiated by Sion in the aftermath of the decision, it was a farcical episode.

Undoubtedly, Celtic would rather have put their opponents to the sword on the pitch but there was no reluctance on Neil Lennon's part at accepting the reprieve. Rules must be adhered to for the purposes of sporting integrity. Celtic followed them. Sion clearly hadn't.

"We played the two games under protest so we always felt, regardless of the result, we would get back in anyway," said the manager. "The first game was disappointing in the fact we didn't score at home, even though we had the majority of the game. In the away match, we lost Daniel Majstorovic in the first minute but I felt we played well enough and we managed to get it back to 2-1. I thought we were going to go on and win it and then we lost a really bad goal. However, we got back in and went into one of the best groups we could have got in terms of quality sides. I felt it really enhanced our season."

Delighted at the opportunity of facing such an array of talented teams, the manager was anxious his players made the most of the experience, and show why they belonged in this illustrious company.

"It meant a lot to me, the backroom staff, the players and the fans to be in this competition," he said. "All we were looking for from the players was to do themselves justice. It's a great competition as far as we're concerned. I was fortunate enough to reach the final of the competition myself and I know what it meant to me personally and my team-mates at the time.

"It was great for our club to be involved in it and for these players to be involved in it. We had a very talented group of young players who could become a very good team if we could keep them together, and this was part of their development. But I didn't want them to take it as a learning curve; I wanted them to go out, play strongly and go forward in the group from there. We had a second chance at the competition so we wanted to make the most of it."

European nights in Paradise are special. The thunderous atmosphere is inspirational for Celtic and intimidating for opponents. Although the Hoops could count on that advantage they had a notoriously poor away record to rectify.

"It was a tough group, with a lot of quality but particularly at home in the European games we should have been able to give these teams a real game," added the Irishman. "Away from home, our record wasn't great, but records are there to be broken and the players had been given a second chance and they wanted to make the most of it.

"It wasn't a huge gulf but it was a big step-up for the players and they would be facing opposition they normally wouldn't face. I just hoped they wouldn't get caught cold. If they went out and mentally focused on the game, the physical aspects would look after themselves."

CELTIC couldn't have asked for a more daunting start to their group campaign – an away fixture at Atletico Madrid. Indeed, the Spanish side would go on to win the Europa League with a resounding 3-0 win over a gifted Athletic Bilbao side in the final. Considering the litany of talent available to the La Liga side, that outcome wasn't a huge surprise

Although stars such as Sergio Aguero and Diego Forlan had left during the summer, they had forked out a reported forty million Euros on prolific Columbian hitman, Falcao, whose goals had helped Porto win the Europa League just months earlier. He may have been the marquee player, but the entire side was packed with an array of international talent with plenty of European experience.

It was also only the second time Celtic had faced Atletico since the infamous European Cup semi-final in 1974 when the Spanish side's thuggish tactics in Paradise had earned them three red cards and a multitude of bookings. Animosity still persisted in some quarters, particularly for several of the Celtic players who had been involved in the fixture. It all added to the pre-match hype. Neil Lennon was relishing the occasion and the challenge.

"We knew the strength-in-depth of Atletico," said the manager. "They had real quality there. They had won this competition in 2010, so the pedigree was up there with any of the clubs in Europe. This was a great challenge for us all and we were looking forward to it.

"Atletico were probably favourites to win it, but with Udinese and Rennes also there, any other year this could have been a Champions League group. We knew it was a huge game. There was going to be a huge jump in quality from what we were used to in the Scottish league, but these were the games we wanted to play in. There are always huge expectations when we play in Scotland, particularly in home games, even in Europe," he added. "This was a change and sometimes it could ease the pressure. We went in as underdogs but there were still expectations from our supporters to put on a performance."

Back in 1974, Celtic had lost the second leg 2-0 in Madrid after the goal-less first-leg battle in Glasgow. That was the same away scoreline in 2011. Living up to his pre-match billing, Falcao headed home from a corner in third minute. He would finish as top scorer in the competition for the second successive season.

Celtic, without Scott Brown and Anthony Stokes through injury, along with the suspended Daniel Majstorovic, mustered up a swift response as a counter-attack presented Gary Hooper with a sight of goal, but he couldn't find a way past the onrushing keeper, Thibaut Courtois. It was the Hoops' best chance of the match. Although the hosts dominated possession, Celtic remained a threat and were a greater attacking force after the break. Ki forced a smart stop from Courtois and Charlie Mulgrew curled a free-kick just past the post. However, midway through the half the home side sealed the points as Arda Turan supplied Diego, who struck an accurate effort beyond Forster.

"We played very well after a poor start," said the Hoops boss. "Losing a goal from a set-piece was very disappointing from our point of view, but we gathered ourselves and straight away we could've equalised through Gary Hooper. The second goal came probably in our best spell of the game. Atletico were an excellent side and you are going to concede possession at times but I thought there had been a lot of very positive performances. We played very well after a poor start and I hoped the players would take something from the performance."

Indeed, despite the defeat in the Vicente Calderon, Celtic had proved they had the wherewithal to compete on this stage. It augured well for the remainder of the group stages and the next game against Udinese at Celtic Park. Overcoming a team who would go on to finish third in Serie A and qualify for the Champions League would be a stiff task, but with support of the Celtic faithful – anything was possible.

"There's no better place on a European night than here at Celtic Park, and the players had to try and set a tempo that the crowd could respond to. When that happens it's normally a great night. It lifts the players' performances and it lifts the team as a whole. Getting that unity around the stadium is fantastic."

The fans were given something to cheer in the third minute as Ki swept Celtic in front from the penalty spot following a foul on Hooper. The hosts remained the most productive team and looked the more likely to add to their lead, with Ki and Hooper both coming close against a youthful Udinese side. Just as it seemed they were about to deservedly collect their first win of group, though, the visitors were awarded a spot-kick in the closing stages. Hooper was harshly penalised for brushing against Udinese's Neutonin in the box. Almen Abdi scored from 12 yards to secure a share of the spoils.

"Gary was very upset and angry, as were all of the players, because they put so much into the game and to lose the three points because of a decision like that was very hard to take," said the manager. "We had controlled the bulk of the game. There were further signs of encouragement. I was delighted with the whole team. People made a lot of Udinese picking a young team, but we had a young team too."

Two games, two decent performances but just the one point to show for it. Celtic needed to start converting their displays into tangible reward. It was a familiar scenario.

DAYS before Celtic jetted off to Rennes for their next Europa League fixture, Neil Lennon had endured the most trying day in his managerial career. Three goals down to Kilmarnock at half-time, the Hoops' season seemed to be spiralling into oblivion. However, they salvaged a draw thanks to a battling display after the break.

The events of the game were still raw. Confidence was fragile. Facing such a formidable side so swiftly could either be construed as terrible timing or a welcome diversion from domestic troubles. The manager took the latter view. This was an opportunity to gather fresh momentum to take into the SPL.

"We had dropped five points in the previous two league games, which wasn't good enough," said the manager. "The players knew that and I knew that. We had two home games coming up and the requirement was maximum points from that and with a good performance into the bargain – that was the main focus for me. I wanted a result in Rennes and I wanted two wins from the next two league games. I wanted us to kick-on."

Nonetheless, this would be a task steeped with difficulty. Rennes had emerged as one of the most vibrant teams in French football over recent years, producing some of the most talented players in the country through their famed youth academy, including French internationalist Y'ann M'Vila. They had plenty of strengths, but there was no fear within the Celtic squad.

"I knew Rennes were an excellent side," Neil Lennon said. "I had watched them myself against Lorient the weekend before we played them and they were very exciting to watch going forward. They were very comfortable at home in the local derby, so they came into the game full of confidence.

"They had plenty of pace in their side. You see different cultures of football – you see the Italian side of it, you see the flair of the Spanish. I think Rennes had a combination of flair, great pace and athleticism in their team, but we had exciting players in our team. We had a young team, a developing team but we believed we could cause Rennes plenty of problems ourselves. We felt we could give them a very strong game and on the back of our second-half performance at Rugby Park, the players went into the game in a good frame of mind."

Occupying bottom spot in the group after two games, collecting some reward from Brittany was vital if Celtic wished to harbour ambitions of qualification to the next stage.

"With the two group leaders playing each other, realistically, we had to try to take something from the game, win our remaining two home games and hope that both leading teams could take points off one another. That would leave the group open for us," the Irishman added.

Celtic went out with that mindset. Anthony Stokes' goalbound shot was saved as Celtic more than matched the home side in an enthralling first half. However, on the stroke of half-time, it looked like all the good work had been undone as the Hoops conceded a calamitous own goal.

A long clearance from the Rennes goalkeeper was flicked on by Cha Du-Ri and the ball ran agonisingly past Forster into the net. Disaster. For teams of lesser character this could have spelled resignation. However, after the break, Celtic fought back and levelled matters as Joe Ledley's header found the far corner from Charlie Mulgrew's free-kick. Forster then atoned for his earlier error with several excellent stops to help Celtic earn a point they thoroughly merited.

"We had a chat with Fraser at half-time, as you can imagine, and he was fantastic. I can't speak highly enough of him," said the manager. "That was exactly the type of reaction I was looking for and he was a great example to the rest of the squad. It was a great way to bounce back and show all the qualities which made us chase him in the summer. The two guys involved in the goal showed great character. Cha had a great second half and Fraser made some wonderful saves. Away from home, no matter who you are, you need your goalkeeper to make some good saves at crucial moments and he did that for us, having come out in the second half probably feeling as low as he could get.

"The goal came from a free-kick we had in a wide area. I wouldn't say it was one of those things – it came from a communication breakdown. You can't legislate for that, no matter how well you prepare the team. The players didn't deserve that and you felt, 'Is this going to happen again?' So it was important to get them in at half-time and settle them down. The reaction was everything I wanted from them and we looked forward to the next three games."

Celtic had shown courage and character in France, but confidence was still fragile as they welcomed Rennes to Paradise for the return meeting. An insipid goal-less draw the previous weekend at home to Hibernian had slowed down domestic momentum. The Hoops now occupied third place in the league behind Motherwell and Rangers, who were stretching away in front. Harvesting wins was becoming critical on both fronts – domestic and European. However, injuries continued to be a recurring problem with Ledley, Ki, Mulgrew and Mark Wilson joining those on the long-term treatment table.

"I still had a good squad of players available and the responsibility lay with them to put in a strong performance. It was going to be a tough game, obviously, but we were all looking forward to it. Every game is important regardless of the competition or the status of where we are in any of the competitions. We wanted to win to keep alive our hopes in the group and then obviously go to Motherwell on Sunday and put on a strong performance.

"We had played very well in Europe – we were unfortunate not to beat Udinese. We played okay in Madrid – I thought we could have played better, but they were a very good side – and in Rennes we were excellent. Rennes were a good counter-attacking side. They were strong and athletic and had some very good footballers in the team, and we had to be wary of that, particularly when we were taking the game to them."

The game started off in the worst possible fashion. Just two minutes had elapsed when Kader Mangane powered a header beyond Forster from a corner. There was still time but this suited a team with Rennes' explosive pace perfectly. They could sit in, frustrate and break swiftly, but Celtic emerged from the depths. Demonstrating determination, resilience and togetherness, they equalised. James Forrest's drive was spilled by Benoit Costil in the Rennes goal and Stokes gobbled up the simple chance. They completed the turnaround before the break through the route one approach. Forster's goal-kick was flicked on by Georgios Samaras, Stokes fastened on to the ball and clinically dispatched a shot into the far corner.

With Loovens unable to continue after the break, seventeen-year-old Marcus Fraser had to deputise in defence in the second half. It was his top-team debut and highlighted the extent of the injury situation. The youngster coped admirably under pressurised circumstances. Celtic successfully repelled the visitors' increasingly desperate attacks before sealing their first win of the group at the death as Gary Hooper finished off an incisive counter-attack.

"It was a wonderful team performance," the manager said. "It was a miracle considering the number of absentees we had. We even lost Glenn Loovens at half-time, which was a blow to us, but Marcus came in and did brilliantly. Georgios Samaras, Anthony Stokes, Beram Kayal and Victor Wanyama were absolutely amazing in midfield. I thought Adam Matthews had a stormer, Daniel Majstorovic was a brick wall in the second half while the goalkeeper made some good saves when we needed him to.

"There were a lot of tired bodies in there and for a young team, it was mentally demanding as well as physically demanding. But against Rennes, as a team we showed real belief in ourselves and I was very proud of the players."

The European adventure was back on track. At the weekend, a revitalised Celtic defeated Motherwell. It was the start of a twenty-game winning sequence.

VICTORY over Rennes had infused Celtic with renewed self-belief. By the time, Atletico Madrid arrived in Glasgow for the penultimate match in the group, the Hoops had strung together a five-game winning sequence – their best of the season to date. Each win was generating greater confidence. The previous weekend, St Mirren had been swept aside in a 5-0 rout in Paradise. It was an altogether rosier picture than prior to the Rennes game.

The pressure was easing on Neil Lennon, the tension surrounding matches was dissipating, but there was still no let-up in focus. The title may have been the overriding priority for the side yet the positive results subsequent to the Rennes triumph signified the significance of success in Europe. This was a match the Hoops were treating with the upmost seriousness.

"The Rennes game was a real shot of confidence and the players never looked back," said the manager. "For all the people who thought we were taking this competition lightly it showed that we weren't. We were pretty serious about it. We want European football at the club. We had enjoyed the challenges so far and had two more big games coming up.

"We had improved in every game in the competition, and the result against St Mirren gave the players a huge shot in the arm going into the game. Winning breeds confidence. I had never questioned the players' commitment, just their consistency, and now we were finding a level of consistency we'd grown in confidence. We found a system that suited us in those games. I believed we had a really good crop of players who were exciting to watch at times and could mix it a bit, but they had to go on and show it."

Four points from the previous two Europa League games had pushed Celtic into a decent position in the group. Another win would give them a wonderful chance of progressing to the knock-out stages. Recent home form boded well, but overcoming the Spanish outfit would require the players to reach new heights.

"We had home advantage and we were in good form off the back of probably our best performance of the season at that point against St Mirren, so it was a game we were really looking forward to," said the Hoops boss. "We could easily have had five against Dunfermline as well and all of a sudden Celtic Park was becoming an intimidating place to come to again, which is exactly what I wanted.

"It was a game we were capable of winning, but there was no com- placency. We couldn't go into it thinking we had cracked it as there

(Above) Supporters show their solidarity with Neil Lennon on the final game of 2010/11 as Celtic miss out on the title by one point; (right) on an emotional day in Paradise, Neil Lennon announces to the crowd that, "this is just the beginning," and then thanks them for their backing

(Above) Head fitness coach, Kenny McMillan, puts the players through their paces to the backdrop of some of Sydney's famous landmarks during pre-season Down Under; (above right) Anthony Stokes is congratulated after scoring Celtic's first goal of the season at Easter Road

(Right) Scott Brown and Wesley Sneijder of Inter Milan exchange words during a fiery friendly at the Dublin Super Cup in July 2011

(Right) Neil Lennon watches grim-faced as Celtic's 100 per cent start to the season ends against St Johnstone

(Left) Paddy McCourt tries to find a way through the FC Sion defence in the Europa League qualifier in Celtic Park

(Below) Agony for Emilio Izaguirre as the influential defender suffers a fractured ankle in the second game of the season at Pittodrie

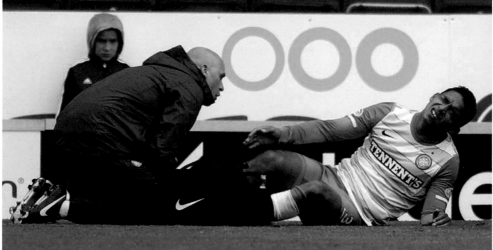

(Above) Another sparkling show from Young Player of the Year, James Forrest, against Motherwell in September

(Above) Ki Sung Yueng opens Celtic's account in the Europa League from the penalty spot in the draw with Udinese

(Right) Worrying times for Neil Lennon as Celtic suffer defeat at Tynecastle in October to fall further behind Rangers

Neil Lennon watches in disbelief and ponders his future as Celtic toil at Rugby Park

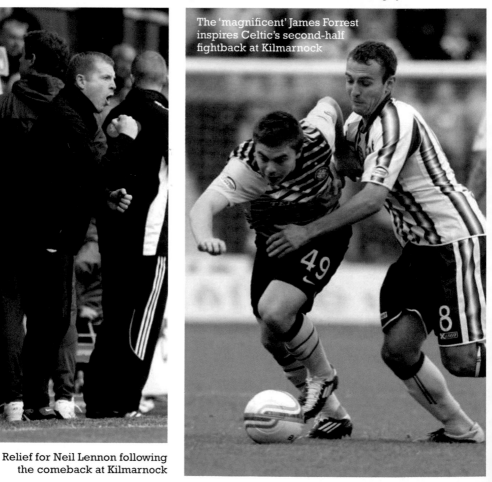

The 'magnificent' James Forrest inspires Celtic's second-half fightback at Kilmarnock

Relief for Neil Lennon following the comeback at Kilmarnock

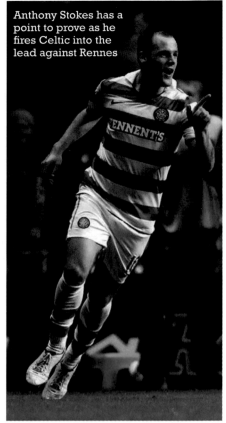

Anthony Stokes has a point to prove as he fires Celtic into the lead against Rennes

(Above) Charlie Mulgrew completes the great escape at Rugby Park, much to the delight of Joe Ledley and the travelling Celtic support; (below) Gary Hooper stabs the ball home to earn Celtic a priceless three points at Motherwell in November

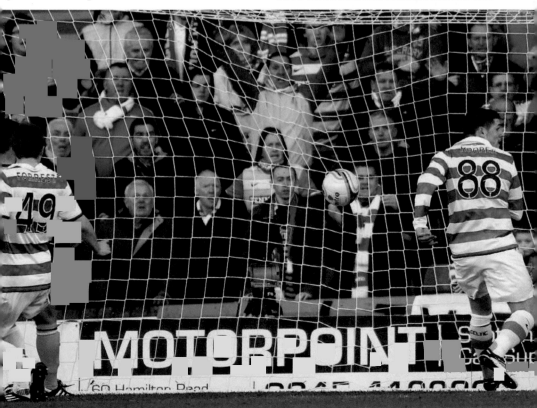

A relieved Neil Lennon celebrates Gary Hooper's late strike in the 'must-win' game at Motherwell in November

(Below) Gary Hooper points to the bench after his late winner at Fir Park – the goal that started the 20-game winning run

Coaching staff congratulate Dylan McGeouch after the teenager scores an incredible solo goal on his Celtic Park bow

(Below) Georgios Samaras in full flight against Atletico Madrid at Celtic Park

Elation as Fraser Forster saves Hearts' last-minute penalty to preserve Celtic's winning run

Joe Ledley is jubilant after scoring the winner against Rangers in December as Celtic stormed to the league summit

James Forrest is mobbed by his team-mates after opening the scoring late in the second half against St Mirren

was still a lot of work to be done. But it was a game that whetted the appetite because I thought it would be open with plenty of football involved. The only thing I had been concerned about was getting good performances from the team, and we were getting that and getting goals. It was a huge test because Atletico Madrid were a class side. They played well against us in the corresponding fixture in Madrid and they had a team packed with quality players.

"We had to be wary of conceding early goals, which we had done in a few of the games in this group so far. We had to get on the front foot and take the game to them. We were under no illusions that it was going to be a tough test for us. There were a few meaty challenges in the first game so I didn't expect Atletico's approach to be light-hearted."

Although Celtic managed to avert falling behind in the opening stages, they still trailed at the break due to Arda Turan's strike on the half-hour mark, the only goal of a keenly-contested first half. Celtic had their chances. Stokes and Daniel Majstorovic both threatened but were foiled by a mixture of stubborn defending and good goalkeeping from Thibault Courtois.

The second half was an enthralling contest as the hosts drove forward in their attempt to restore parity, while Atletico remained menacing on the break. Ki forced Courtois into a smart stop with a rasping free-kick, before Gary Hooper thought he had levelled matters – but his goal was ruled out for a handball by Stokes in the build-up. A frantic late push for an equaliser proved in vain as the Spaniards held out for the three points and clinch their spot in the next round. They had shown some of the reasons why they would go all the way in the tournament. Nonetheless, Celtic deserved more from the game.

"I thought we matched them for most of the game, if not better them," said the manager. "It was an excellent performance and I thought we deserved better from it. We came up against an excellent side that defended and counter-attacked very well, but I could only give credit to the players for having a good go at it. I had seen a gradual progression and improvement in all the performances and this was a great stage to play in for these players."

The reversal meant Celtic had to beat Udinese in their final group match on December 15 if they wished to join Atletico in the knockout stages, an extremely challenging assignment. Since the last meeting of the sides, the Italian outfit had risen to the Serie A summit, alongside Juventus, and this time they couldn't afford to rest any stars such as Antonio Di Natale, given what was at stake. Celtic's poor away record in European competition didn't exactly auger well either.

"It was a tall order," said the manager. "Udinese were an excellent side and we hadn't won away from home in a long while but we gave it everything we had. We had to win it. A draw or a defeat was no good to us. We had to be very respectful of the opposition who were top of Serie A, so they were obviously an excellent side. They played a different formation to what we were accustomed to.

"It was hard to tell what Udinese's best team was because they had such a strong squad. But whatever side we faced it would be top-class opposition who were intent on qualifying from the group themselves. They were very strong in midfield. They had great strength, athleticism and quality, and they counter-attacked very quickly.

"Added to that, they had a brilliant goalkeeper in Samir Handanovic. I think he is one of the best in the world. I remembered him from the last World Cup for Slovenia and he was fantastic, he pulled off three or four unbelievable saves at Celtic Park. He gave them a great foundation for them to build on, and with people like Di Natale in the team, there was always a goal threat at the other end. They were very well-organised but skilful into the bargain."

Nonetheless, Celtic also had reasons to be cheerful. They were in the midst of an impressive winning domestic run and were brimming with confidence. It was a completely different team to the one Udinese had faced in Glasgow. Furthermore, not many gave the Hoops much hope of success. The pressure was off, allowing them to perform with greater freedom.

"I thought we could set up to be a little bit more adventurous with our own approach," the manager said. "The pressure was off and the players could go and hopefully express themselves and do the club justice. We were in good form off the back of six wins in the league and confidence was good in the squad. In each of those Europa games there had been a gradual progression of improvement within the team. They were learning all the time and we treated it like a cup final. It was a great game to play in and it was a great incentive for the players. It was one they were all looking forward to."

Given the formidable make-up of the group, having qualification in their own hands in the final round of fixtures was a decent achievement in itself for Celtic.

"It was always going to be a difficult group, and the calibre of the other teams in it, alongside ourselves, were of Champions League quality," explained the Hoops boss. "We were a developing team, however, and I think going into this group, a lot of outsiders would have made us the whipping boys. But we had been very pleased with how the team had played in the five games, and the fact we were still in with a shout of qualifying going into the last game was testament to the players."

The hosts soon realised this wouldn't be a straightforward evening. Celtic began with purpose and determination, taking the game to the Serie A side. James Forrest tried his luck from distance, before Hooper was agonisingly close to the opener, shooting wide after a wonderful pass from Samaras. At the other end, Di Natale was a constant threat and was narrowly off target with a chip after latching on to a short back-pass from Scott Brown, who was making his first start following a long-lay off. As the half-hour mark approached, the visitors shocked the home crowd by going in front. Samaras drove down the left and his driven cross ricocheted around the six-yard box. It dropped invitingly for Hooper and he tapped home. This was not in the script. Stung by that blow, the home side poured forward and got their reward before the break. There was no surprise at who dished out the punishment as Di Natale clinically finished on the volley when Celtic failed to clear.

The second half was end-to-end as Celtic pressed for a winner and Udinese replied on the counter-attack. Fraser Forster came to the Hoops' rescue on several occasions with some terrific stops, including an incredible double-save, while only the width of the post denied Cha Du-Ri a goal. Despite a late push from Celtic, and a late penalty claim, the winner never arrived and the home support breathed a huge sigh of relief at the final whistle. Ultimately, the Hoops were out of the Europa League and there was natural disappointment at that outcome but it had been a stirring effort. There had been some good displays over the six games but the best had certainly been reserved for last.

Playing with poise, control and composure, Celtic had made significant strides throughout the European campaign. They looked like they belonged in this company, which was no mean feat. The Hoops resumed domestic duties brimming with a self-belief which would help them maintain their winning momentum for a further two months.

"It was up there as one of the best performances in my time in management, certainly away from home in Europe against probably the best team that I have faced," said the manager. "All credit to Udinese, you could see why they were up there [in Serie A], but we felt we were a pretty good side ourselves. I took a lot of positives from the game. From the first whistle to the death I thought we were fantastic as a team and there were some wonderful performances.

"Fraser went out and expressed himself. We had said to him he might be busy and asked if he could make the saves when he needed to and he certainly did that. The double-save, I just thought that was a goal. He was improving all the time. Forrest, Samaras and Hooper as a front three were excellent but the team as a whole was the star on the night. We were very unfortunate not to go through. To come and play a team at the top of Serie A and take the game to them and play the football we played and create the chances we created – I couldn't speak highly enough of the team. Now we had to transmit that from European football to domestic honours."

6

Neighbourhood
Watch

THE combustible atmosphere of a Glasgow derby is no place for the faint-hearted. It requires people who possess passion, determination and a fierce will to win – people like Neil Lennon. Ever since arriving in Glasgow in December 2000 from Leicester City, the Irishman has been involved in some epic derby duels first as a player and now as a manager. On the field, he relished the encounters – the noise, the frenzy and the intensity. He loved to win. He hated to lose. He was a Celtic supporter. He knew what the fixture meant.

Nothing changed when he stepped into the managerial hot-seat. This time, however, there was a greater weight of responsibility on his shoulders. It was a heavy burden to carry. There was no gentle introduction in his first full season in charge. Far from it. He took charge of Celtic in no fewer than seven of these highly-charged fixtures in the space of seven months – four in the league and three in the cups, including a League Cup final. With both sides fighting a desperate and closely-contested struggle for the title throughout 2010/11, every match took on even greater significance, if that were possible.

Along the way he experienced every emotion – elation, frustration, tension, anguish. It was an exhausting process. There was still the same jubilation of victory he felt as a player, but it was now accompanied by an overwhelming sensation of relief as the pressure abated, for that brief moment.

"As a player, you really look forward to it. Managing, you hate it," he explained. "You have that dry mouth and a feeling in the pit of your stomach for a couple of days. If you win it's great, if you lose it's horrendous. The build-up is all hyped up and the fall-out is all hyped up. You try and keep a level head going into these games but it's difficult sometimes as it means so much to so many people.

"You are the manager and if you win everyone starts going on about your tactics and everything, but it's all about the players on the day. If they're in the right frame of mind, if they play with the right intensity and quality, you will win more than you lose. When you win, there is relief and satisfaction and you feel quite happy. You enjoy it for a day but then you need to start thinking about the next game. If you lose, you sit and sulk for two or three days in a dark room and then you have to pick yourself up and go again."

In season 2011/12, the great rivals would 'only' meet on four occasions during the campaign – perhaps a blessing for all those to fully recover from the excitement of the previous season – but there would be no decline in drama, controversy and excitement. It was a tale of mixed fortunes. Celtic won both home games but suffered disappointment on their two visits to Ibrox. Perhaps the most frustrating factor was the Hoops' slow start in the first three fixtures.

"It looks as if it's a case of home and away," said the Irishman. "We didn't start the first three games that well at all for my liking but I thought we had good control in the home games. I thought in the first derby at Ibrox, we fortunately went in at half-time a goal up but I felt we had deserved to get the equaliser as we played quite well after Naismith had scored early on. Then we didn't turn up in the second half and didn't compete and Rangers thoroughly deserved to win it on the day. The second game in December, again, we didn't start well but after we found our feet we were comfortable winners, even though it was only 1-0.

"We didn't start the third game well at Ibrox. Aluko scored a fine individual goal but then Sammi went on a great run and the ball came out to Anthony and we felt he should have done better, and then McGregor has made a great save from him. We then lost Cha to the red card and we had to sacrifice Anthony for that. So it wasn't a great day for us. We showed great character to come back with nine men and get a couple of goals.

"In the last home game we were very comfortable. It was as good as we had played against Rangers for a while. It was a fantastic performance and everything I wanted from the team they gave me that day."

On the basis of the two reversals, Ibrox wasn't a venue with many fond memories for the manager, notwithstanding the hostile reception he always receives there from the home support. This has been a constant, if depressing, theme throughout his association with Celtic. Nonetheless, despite these adverse conditions, he actually relished trips to Rangers' home ground.

"I don't mind it at all," he said. "I enjoy the games. They are great occasions and I like actually Ibrox as a stadium. It's always a decent pitch to play on. The atmosphere is always quite intense but I quite enjoy those situations."

There wasn't a long wait before his first instalment of the season. In September, seven matches into the campaign, Celtic headed to Ibrox for the first derby day of the 2011/12. At that point, little separated the teams. Ally McCoist's side held a slender one-point advantage. A win for either side would provide a confidence boost but wouldn't strike a fatal blow in the race for the championship.

The build-up to the game wasn't ideal for Celtic. While a comprehensive 4-0 win over Motherwell a week earlier ranked among the Hoops' most impressive performances of the season, it was outweighed by the demands of midweek Europa League duty.

Three days before the trip to Govan, Celtic had succumbed to a 2-0 defeat to Atletico Madrid in the Spanish heat. It had been a gruelling exercise against a team proficient in retaining possession. The team landed back in Glasgow on Friday, leaving less than forty-eight hours recovery time for the game at Ibrox. Still, spirits were high after a commendable display against the La Liga outfit.

"I was hoping the players would take something from their performance in Madrid," said the manager. "The game at Ibrox was one they were relishing, and I was looking for a similar kind of display. I didn't think there would be any hangover for Sunday's game. We also had to be careful with a few players like Scott Brown and Anthony Stokes, who didn't travel, but we also had a couple of players who hadn't played for five or six weeks like Mark Wilson and Glenn Loovens, and they had acquitted themselves very well. We had the players in on Saturday morning but it was very light, and the momentum from the game on Thursday should have been there for them to take into Sunday."

It would mean two games of huge significance in the space of four days, but the Hoops boss wasn't complaining.

"For a club like ours to be playing Atletico Madrid and then Rangers in the space of three or four days was fantastic," he said. "The players were all looking forward to it. You've got the adrenalin and the momentum with you. You just go out and play those games and you get a rhythm about you. We approached this one like we approach every game. We tried to be positive and win the game but we also had to be very strong mentally, and be ready for anything that Rangers might throw at us."

It was the hosts who made the early running and they opened the scoring midway through the half through Steven Naismith. A cross from the left was only cleared as far as the Scottish internationalist and he volleyed into the top corner past Fraser Forster. That spurred Celtic into action and they levelled the match through Gary Hooper just over ten minutes later. The striker fastened on to Scott Brown's precise pass and curled a controlled shot into the far corner from an acute angle. It was a wonderful finish.

Before the break, the Bhoys scored again. Badr El Kaddouri was the unlikely source of the goal. The Moroccan picked up a pass from Ki Sung Yueng and unleashed a shot on target. It should have been simple fare for Allan McGregor but he contrived to allow the ball to slip from his grasp and trundle over the line.

Instead of Celtic driving home their superiority in the second half, however, the Ibrox side took charge of proceedings. Nikica Jelavic headed home from a corner to equalise. Celtic were a matter of inches from taking the lead again as Glenn Loovens' header thumped off the post, and Rangers capitalised on the missed opportunity as Kyle Lafferty put them in front, bundling home from close-range.

Charlie Mulgrew saw red for a second booking as the Hoops' day went from bad to worse, and then the ten men were punished on the counter-attack as Naismith added a second in the last minute. Three unanswered goals in the second half told their own story.

"We had gone in at half-time 2-1 up, albeit fortuitously with the second goal, and I told the players to be careful for the next 10-15 minutes. But in the second half we never competed at all and that was really disappointing from my point of view. We were pleased to be ahead at half-time, which was a bonus because I would have been pleased with 1-1. We had felt comfortable. But we didn't deal with the second half well at all.

"If we had stayed in front for the first ten or fifteen minutes of the second half we could probably have gone on to cause a few more problems at their end of the pitch, but we never got out of the block. You have to earn your right to play and we did that in the first half, got our foothold in the game and got a bit of luck with the second goal, but we competed. We were good defensively, and the goalkeeper didn't have too much to do in the first half. In the second half, though, the warning signs were there when Davis hit the bar but we didn't take any heed from it and we lost the physical battle. It was very frustrating. We hit the post from a corner and Rangers went up the other end and scored so that was probably the game-changing moment."

Put simply, it was not up to standard and the manager let the players know this in no uncertain terms.

"It wasn't devastating but it was concerning," he added. "I wasn't happy with them and I left them in no uncertain terms as to what I thought of them that day."

DEFEAT in the first derby of the season had been disappointing but not decisive. Celtic's victory in the second meeting of the sides in late December helped determine the destiny of their season.

"That was a pivotal game as it was the first time we went ahead of them in the league and we never looked back after that," said the manager. "You could just feel that the momentum was with us. On the night I thought we controlled the game very well in difficult conditions and with a bit of luck we could have won the game a bit more comfortably."

Having fallen fifteen points behind their great rivals at one stage, Celtic had launched an incredible comeback to claw back the gap to just one point in the space of eight weeks. They had the momentum, Rangers were stuttering. The Hoops had won eight games on the spin in contrast to the Ibrox side's indifferent form, harvesting only ten points from their previous six games.

A ninth successive triumph for Celtic would see them leapfrog Ally McCoist's side on to the SPL summit by the end of the year, completing a remarkable turnaround. While the prize of victory would be incentive enough for each team, this game had wider implications for the title race, and both sides knew it. With home advantage and the confidence from an impressive run of victories to draw upon, Celtic were saddled with the favourites tag. However, they couldn't afford to let standards drop, particularly not for this one.

"We wanted to make home advantage count and keep the winning run going," said the manager, "but Rangers are always dangerous opponents, regardless of timing. We were looking to go from strength to strength. We'd had a rough period. It wasn't nice and it wasn't nice for me in terms of the disappointment I was getting from the results, but that's part of football and you had to accept that sometimes. But we had found a consistency. The players were playing to the form we knew that they could and we just hoped it could continue. It was our job to make sure that it did."

After the customary pre-match hype and build-up, the match nearly never got underway. As stormy winds battered the West of Scotland, a panel on one of the the big screens at Celtic Park became loose and there was a race against time for repairs to be completed. Thankfully for the Hoops, the game was given the green light.

The wild weather conditions matched the action on the pitch as the game began at a furious tempo. Both sides fought hard for supremacy. The first meaningful chance fell to the visitors when Lee

Wallace stooped to head Sone Aluko's cross on target. Fraser Forster sprang to his right, though, and somehow clawed the ball to safety. Rangers claimed the ball had crossed the line but to no avail. Scott Brown then forced Allan McGregor into action at the other end as the hosts began to look more menacing. Georgios Samaras believed he had made the breakthrough, converting the rebound after Gary Hooper's powerful shot was saved by McGregor. The raised linesman's flag halted the celebrations, however.

Celtic began the second half with purpose and intent, dominating possession and territory, and deservedly took the lead on fifty-two minutes courtesy of Joe Ledley. McGregor had saved James Forrest's rasping drive at the expense of a corner, and the Welshman headed home Charlie Mulgrew's delivery at the far post. The Hoops were in complete control and Celtic Park was rocking. Wanyama and Brown sent efforts over, while Forrest failed to connect with Samaras' cutback as the hosts threatened to double their advantage. Much to Hooper's frustration, he was incorrectly flagged for offside when bearing down on goal.

Still, one goal proved to be enough as Celtic comfortably repelled the visitors' attempts to force an equaliser, and their growing frustration was manifested in the closing stages through two reckless challenges from David Healy and Kyle Lafferty. For the first time since the opening weeks of the season, Celtic occupied the SPL summit. From that moment on, they wouldn't be moved from that perch. Neil Lennon was proud of his players.

"Psychologically it was huge, going into the New Year having been so far behind to being a point ahead gave the players massive confidence," reflected the manager. "It gave the club a huge lift as well and we never really looked back after that. The important thing was to win and to make it nine in a row. It was the best Christmas and New Year I could have asked for. I was so proud of the players. I kept believing in the players and we turned it around, although there was still a long way to go in the season."

The result maintained the winning run for Neil Lennon's men and gave them a two-point lead over their Glasgow rivals. From Celtic's dominance of the second forty-five minutes, there was little doubt that they deserved the victory.

"In the second half I didn't think we were under that much pressure, and I was just delighted to get the goal when we did. We had tried to pick a team that could win the game and I thought our control was good, particularly in the second half. I didn't think we passed the ball quickly enough in the first half, and I didn't think there was much in the game at that point. Kayal was brilliant, and I thought Rogne and Mulgrew had fantastic games. Forrest too, was a great out-ball for us."

It was a pivotal point in the title race but there's always a sense of satisfaction at taking the spoils against your rivals. The reversal at Ibrox earlier in the season remained a sore point for the Hoops boss.

"I had been waiting for three months for this game because the 4-2 defeat really hurt me, particularly the second half. I wanted a response, and I got that," he said. "We had beaten some really good teams in that phase and we had had some really good performances. I had felt a bit for Ki, Stokes and Cha because I couldn't pick everyone, but they had played their part in the run and they would play a part again."

THE moment is etched on the minds of every Celtic supporter. Collecting a throw-in on the right, Jimmy Johnstone spins inside and cuts a path across the thick, muddy Ibrox surface towards the box. He swings a left foot at the ball as a Rangers defender makes a last, desperate lunge to block the shot. It's in vain. The connection is perfect. The ball flies through the torrential rain and slams into the top corner before bouncing to the ground and sticking in the churned-up muck around the goalmouth. Euphoria. 'Jinky' is mobbed by his delirious team-mates and then raises his arms aloft in joy – an iconic Celtic image.

It was May 6, 1967, and this was the goal which secured the championship for Celtic in their season of glory, when they won every competition they entered, including the European Cup.

It was also the last time the Hoops had been crowned champions at the home of their old foes. Nearly forty-five years later, on March 25, 2012, they were presented with the opportunity of repeating that achievement, a fanciful prospect just a few months earlier when Celtic trailed Rangers by a considerable distance in the championship race.

However, on the back of twenty successive wins in domestic football, the Bhoys had gone on to amass an enormous twenty-one-point advantage over the stuttering Ibrox side, who had also suffered a ten-point deduction for entering administration. Motherwell's failure to extract full points against Kilmarnock the previous day meant Celtic could seal the title at Ibrox. It was impossible to overlook during the build-up but the focus for Celtic was simply on winning the game.

"We always want to go and win a derby and that one was no different," said the manager. "It's a great fixture and when they are first drawn it's the one everyone looks forward to. The build-up to this one was no different to any other. The only preparation we made was to get the boys ready to win a game of football. If that meant winning the title as a result then so be it. We were going there to play a football game and to try to win it and if we did that then great. If we didn't we would move on to the next one.

"If we had won the title we would have enjoyed the moment. We wouldn't be there to gloat but we would have celebrated among ourselves and then looked forward to the home game against St Johnstone where we could have really relaxed and enjoyed what we had achieved. We had plenty of time to celebrate in the upcoming games. The last thing we wanted to do was rub it in people's faces. We would be respectful of everyone at the stadium."

Potential party planning ranked at the bottom of the Irishman's list of priorities.

"I didn't like talking about winning games and winning titles because there was still a lot of football to be played before we could achieve that," he added.

That had particular resonance at the time. One week earlier, Celtic had fallen to a shock defeat in the League Cup final to Kilmarnock. No one was looking further ahead than events on the pitch. Five goals and four red cards later, there were plenty of these to digest.

Having exited the Scottish Cup to Dundee United in their previous match, Rangers' chances of winning silverware in 2011/12 had vanished. Arguably, this match had morphed into their most significant one of the season, reflected in the brisk start they made. In the 11th minute, they opened the scoring. Sone Aluko collected possession deep inside Celtic territory and skipped past several challenges, before slipping the ball under Fraser Forster.

It was a superb individual effort from the Nigerian but Samaras almost surpassed that as Celtic mounted a rapid response. The Greek striker embarked on a purposeful run from inside his own half. He skilfully evaded four challenges, giving him a clear sight of goal but Allan McGregor managed to block his effort. The rebound fell to Stokes, but he failed to make a proper connection. He did so with a dipping volley shortly after but McGregor was equal to the task once again. It was entertaining fare. Both teams were posing an attacking threat. However, a controversial red card awarded to Cha Du-Ri close to half-time halted Celtic's momentum.

"Aluko had scored a great individual goal," reflected the manager. "It was brilliant but then we created one or two good chances at the other end. Sammi went on a wonder run and had a shot blocked, then

Stokes sclaffed a volley. He then had another volley that McGregor tipped round the post which was absolutely marvellous. Scott Brown put a great cross to the far post and Stoksey probably could have done better with the header but we were well in the game, as were Rangers. We were both creating chances, and the sending off changed that."

The South Korean was penalised for pulling back Lee Wallace on the edge of the box and was deemed by referee, Calum Murray, to have been the last man. It was an extremely harsh decision.

"I don't think Wallace was ever getting the ball and the contact by Cha was minimal," said the Hoops boss. "Even if he had got the ball it wasn't a clear-cut goalscoring opportunity so I couldn't believe he was sent off. It was a yellow card at best. We had changed it after about 10-15 minutes and went to the diamond which suited us – we started creating chances. We had wanted to weather the storm, and it was disappointing to give the goal away, but after that we were fine.

"We were in the game, working the goalkeeper and it looked like we had settled, and then the sending off changed that. For me it wasn't a sending off. The way the game was going it could have ebbed and flowed either way – the chances we were creating, the changes Rangers were creating."

Despite the direness of their predicament, Neil Lennon certainly wasn't downcast at half-time – with good reason. Celtic had faced the exact same scenario at Ibrox twelve months earlier in a Scottish Cup quarter-final tie. On that occasion the Hoops trailed 2-1 at the break, with Fraser Forster receiving his marching orders. Nevertheless, they dominated the second half and deservedly rescued a replay thanks to a stunning goal from Scott Brown.

"Even at half-time, I thought, 'We've been here before'," said the manager. "We were here in a cup tie last year, down to ten men and a goal down and played very well in the second half. I was looking forward to the second half, getting a response from the team."

Victor Wanyama's red card in the 56th minute for a two-footed tackle on Steven Whittaker rendered Celtic's task almost impossible. Helped by a series of excellent saves from Forster, the nine men held out for another sixteen minutes when Andy Little doubled the home side's advantage from close range, although Lee Wallace appeared offside in the build-up to the goal.

Rangers made it 3-0 through Wallace as the gaps grew in the Celtic defence. Game over – or was it? Bravely, the Hoops continued to push forward and nearly completed an amazing escape. In the 89th minute, Scott Brown converted from a penalty after Samaras had been brought down by Carlos Bocanegra, the third player to see red. In added time, Thomas Rogne headed home from a free-kick. It was a valiant effort but too late. The clock was against the Bhoys. The title party would have to wait.

"We didn't pass the ball as well as we could have but we were 1-0 down, with ten men, just like we were last year," said the manager. "We came back on that occasion and we knew we were capable this time as well. We had a right good go but we knew it wasn't to be. Victor's sending off was debatable. I know he got plenty of the ball, but if you tackle two-footed it's an invitation for a referee. I didn't have too many complaints about that one. He will learn from that, you can't tackle like that. Rangers' second goal was offside and for the third we were caught chasing the game, but we rallied brilliantly – with nine men – which was absolutely fantastic."

While pleased with his players' character, the manager was dismayed over his treatment by the match officials after being sent off at the interval. For security reasons, he was unable to watch the remainder of the game from the Main Stand at Ibrox. Instead he was forced to view it on TV from the confines the press room, a huge impediment on him carrying out his normal duties. A later hearing at Hampden imposed no further punishment.

"The fourth official had a quiet word with me, which was fine, and I had a quiet word, coldly, with the referee going up the tunnel at half-time," explained the Irishman. "I did my team-talk, I came back out and found out I had been sent off and was told I wasn't allowed to go back out. I was absolutely raging with that because I was being deprived of doing my job. It was a huge disappointment but I got a fair hearing and we do feel vindicated that our behaviour was of an appropriate standard.

"As is normal in the aftermath of these games, I was guilty until proved innocent, and not the other way around as it is for everyone else," he added. "The hearing allowed us to give our take on it and we were quite happy with the way things went. We were pleased to have no extra sanction from the Ibrox game."

Disappointed by the result yet proud of the players and supporters, it's a game which evokes a range of emotions.

"Regardless of Rangers winning the game, and we congratulated them on that, it was the manner in which the game went that I was angry about," said the manager. "I was very proud of my players and the supporters, though. The character they showed in the second half told me they would be champions sooner rather than later. We don't expect to win when we go to Ibrox but I'm disappointed in the manner in which it was lost. We came back and rallied brilliantly, which I've seen us do a lot this season, but unfortunately we were talking about things which surround the game. I felt very aggrieved that I wasn't able to do my job properly in the second half."

BY the time of the final derby of the season, Celtic had been crowned champions. Neil Lennon and the players had nothing to prove. They were worthy winners of the title by any measure, a fact confirmed by the emphatic gap between the Hoops and the rest of the SPL in the table, along with their incredible winning sequence which put them in that commanding position.

Nonetheless, this was a Glasgow derby and Celtic wanted to beat their rivals in front of their own supporters at Paradise. While the hype machine went into typical overdrive ahead of the encounter – for a number of reasons – the manager and squad remained calm, impassive and focused on winning the match. An impressive 3-0 triumph over Motherwell the previous weekend had been a welcome boost after the defeat to Hearts in the Scottish Cup semi-final. Now the key was maintaining that level of performance.

"The mood was very good," said the manager. "We had had a great result the weekend before. I just wanted us to win the game – play well, win the game and move on to the next game."

The recent 3-2 defeat at Ibrox did, of course, remain vivid for the squad. Avenging that loss was certainly a source of incentive.

"The players knew themselves they could do better and I was sure they would be very motivated to do that," added the Hoops boss.

Because of his touchline ban, sustained during the Scottish Cup semi-final defeat to Hearts, the Irishman was restricted to watching the events from a seat in the Main Stand at Celtic Park. It was certainly an improvement on the media room at Ibrox – his vantage point in the second half for the last derby game – but it wasn't ideal for a game of such magnitude.

"Any game you have to sit in the stand and watch is difficult, but we had prepared the team very well the previous week and we had done the same for this one," he said. "Sometimes you just have to trust the players and just say, 'Go and do it.' I have good backroom staff here so they can take care of things and we just needed to make sure the players were in the right frame of mind to go and play the way they could."

Their manager may have been absent on the touchline but his

passion, will-to-win and determination were evident among his players on the pitch. From the first whistle, they set about their task with vigour, working tirelessly all over the pitch to win the individual battles, and were rewarded in the 17th minute as Charlie Mulgrew opened the scoring from a well-worked set-piece. Kris Commons swung a deep corner to the far post and it was met by the head of the onrushing defender, who sent a powerful diving header beyond Allan McGregor.

"The set-piece was something we looked at," said the manager. "We just felt there was an area there we could exploit at the back post if we took all the best headers of the ball away from that area. But, again, Kris has got to execute the cross and Charlie's got to put it away so it gave us a great foothold in the game."

Spurred on by their early breakthrough, a fluid and confident Celtic grew in ascendancy and doubled their advantage before the break. Again, there was plenty to admire in the execution of the goal. Gary Hooper picked up possession on the right and fed a perfectly-weighted pass into Commons. With the Rangers defence in disarray, the midfielder skipped past one challenge before calmly chipping the ball over the advancing McGregor. Incredibly, it was his first goal of the season – but it had been worth the wait.

"The second goal was brilliant as there was a great pass from Gary and Kris has drawn his marker in and then got away from him," said the manager. "It was a great finish because they're not easy. They look easy but they're not. We hadn't started games against Rangers in the first three matches of the season so it was imperative that we got a foothold in this one early. Our central midfield, Brown and Ledley, were fantastic. They covered every blade of grass and read the game very well. They broke the play up and got the ball into Commons, who was exceptional in the game as well. So they did everything we had asked them to do and I was so proud of them."

There was no let-up in Celtic's intensity after the restart. McGregor gratefully smothered the ball after a melee in the six-yard box, before turning Joe Ledley's strike over the bar. However, he could do nothing about the third goal. Commons won possession deep in Rangers territory and Georgios Samaras' accurate pass found Hooper in full flight, who duly rifled a venomous first-time shot high into the net. The vast majority of Paradise was in delirium.

Having completed the hard work, the hosts comfortably saw out the remainder of a one-sided match. It was convincing, the display of champions. The nonsensical notion that Celtic couldn't deliver on the big occasion following the defeats at Hampden and at Ibrox had been established as entirely groundless.

"I look back on that game with great joy and satisfaction," said the manager. "I was very happy with the performance and the style of football we played. The quality of the goals was magnificent along with the attitude and application from start to finish. It was an emphatic performance. The players answered all their critics and silenced them with that performance.

"People had thrown the accusation at us that we couldn't handle the big games so that would have diminished after this game. I was very proud of the team. I was very proud of the way they played, the way they passed the ball and we had three great goals. Things that we worked on at the training ground came to fruition and we had changed the system to maybe suit some of the better players. There was real intensity. We had got the whole package. That's not easy going into those pressurised situations.

"There was a great belief about the team and great composure on the ball at times, and great pace, particularly in the wide areas from Adam and Emilio. We were able to keep the pitch big and exploit the areas in which we felt we could. We got off to a good start with the set-piece and after that we never looked back. It was just a good day, a really good day, although we didn't need it, because we were the champions and we had lost one game in the league since October so the media had set really high standards if they thought that we were bottle merchants."

All three goals had been carefully constructed and finished with finesse. It was hard to find any fault with the display.

"They were all brilliant goals and at 3-0 I was thinking I just don't want Rangers to score and get back into the game – although everybody else was probably thinking about four or five goals," added the Irishman. "I had no complaints whatsoever as we had been brilliant from start to finish. Once we had found our feet in the game we were magnificent. I couldn't ask any more of the team. They've answered all the questions and they showed they are worthy champions."

The result, the performance and the atmosphere drew comparisons with the memorable 3-0 triumph at Celtic Park the previous season.

"Every derby win is great," said the Hoops boss. "We played some great football last year and it was very similar – even the atmosphere was very similar. I thought our supporters were magnificent and looked like they really enjoyed the occasion as well."

Rangers' grim financial situation had raised the idea that this could have been the final clash of the big two, if not forever, then for some considerable time. Celtic had won the first-ever match between the two sides 5-2 back in May 1888. Could they have won the last one as well? Only time would tell.

"As a player you'd miss them terribly but as a manager they're horrible," said the Irishman "Honestly, even in this match, when there was no real pressure on the game, you were still always apprehensive going into it. The build-up starts a week in advance and then there's the fallout after it, with the press saying I got the tactics bang on, the team was up for it and all that nonsense.

"We had played well in the match, we had been the better team and proved to be champions, but don't buy into all the tactical stuff in that

I got one over on him or he got one over on me. We had just won the game on the day and I was thrilled with that."

Campaign Supernova

AS the final whistle sounded at Rugby Park, Neil Lennon experienced a rush of emotions – elation, delight and relief. Above all, he felt a sense of immense pride. He was a championship-winning manager of Celtic Football Club. That meant everything to him. Despite all his previous achievements in the game, the Irishman knew delivering the title was essential in proving he deserved to be in charge of Celtic. Mission accomplished.

No longer was he in the shadow of the legendary managers who had brought league titles to Paradise – the likes of Willie Maley, Jimmy McGrory, Jock Stein, Billy McNeill, Davie Hay, Wim Jansen, Martin O'Neill and Gordon Strachan. He had now earned his place alongside that exalted company. Now when he walked past the reminders of their great successes which adorn the corridors of Celtic Park, he could hold his head high.

When he signed for Celtic, the club he had supported since

childhood, it was the fulfilment of a lifelong dream. As a player and then captain, he achieved terrific success, winning every domestic honour in Scottish football, but being appointed manager was a massive privilege. It was something very special. Leading the team to a title triumph, however, surpassed them all.

"This meant everything," he said. "It was the best day in my professional life. I came here in 2000 under Martin and for the last two years had felt like I was on probation. People were maybe unsure if I was justified in being the Celtic manager because I was so inexperienced, but they were going to have to take me more seriously now. There's a lot more substance than a lot of people think. You dream about being a player, you dream about being a captain and you dream about being a manager, but I was now living the dream.

"When you're a player, you are part of a team. I had Larsson, Sutton, Petrov, Lambert, Mjallby and Thompson to lean on. When you're the manager, it is a lonely job, you have to make the decisions. I was only young in this job. It was only my second season. It's a huge job with huge expectations, but I felt vindicated. We should have enjoyed it. It was our first one in four years. I had won a few championships but this meant more to me than any of the others because I was the manager. You have to find a lot of answers, but it's all worth it in the end. To walk alongside Mr Stein, Billy McNeill, Davie Hay, Wim Jansen, Martin and Gordon was a very special feeling."

Unlike his predecessors, the Irishman had been subject to an unprecedented campaign of hatred and intimidation during his two years in the post. It had placed a huge strain on his personal life, notwithstanding the normal football pressures of being in the Celtic hot-seat. That made it an even greater personal triumph.

"There are things outside the football that have affected my life and it's not always an easy thing to deal with," he said. "It obviously takes a bit of strength to get through it but it takes a bit of support as well and

I had great support from my family, the players, the club, the board, Mr Desmond and Peter Lawwell, in particular. They had thrown everything at me but I'm now, after twelve years with this club, at the pinnacle of my professional career, so I wasn't going to go away in a hurry. It had been an emotional two years for me. To finish it off the way we did was brilliant."

After the agony of missing out on the title by one point twelve months earlier in his first season at the helm, the manager had been desperate to go one better this time around. He had succeeded, though it had been a huge test of character and nerve.

"It's a day you dream about in your mind and we came so close last year," he added. "You just never know what happens in football. You think that might have been your chance gone but we were all very determined to go one better this year."

At one stage, it all seemed a remote possibility. Celtic were fifteen points behind Rangers at the start of November and were even outside the top two places in the table. Some doubted whether that gap could be closed, though not the manager. His only surprise was how swiftly they did it. A seventeen-game winning sequence in the league saw them leapfrog Rangers by the turn of the year.

"It was a marathon, not a sprint," he said. "Even when we were fifteen points behind in October, I believed we could get back into it. I said that to the players, that if we could just chip away three points a month, we would catch them by April, plus we still had to play them three times. I didn't envisage we could close the gap so quickly but the psychology of the environment turned very quickly and all the momentum started to come with us – but we still had to go out and win the games and we did that very well."

Throughout all the trials and tribulations, the highs and the lows, the manager insisted that he maintained the same mindset.

"Whoever we play, other than Rangers, the other team is the

underdog and the expectation level is to win. If you win it's expected. If you lose or draw, it's a national disaster. Then the criticism comes, but it's all just hype. I had been here a long time and I knew I just had to keep a level head. You go through the bad times and get things thrown at you and you have to accept it for what it is. When you go on a winning run and people are starting to pat you on the back and say that your team is brilliant, then you must keep a level head as well and just keep looking for the dangers which are around the corner.

"Obviously, through the difficult times we were scratching our heads and trying to come up with answers. We found them in the end. We take defeat very badly. We enjoy the wins for a brief period and then prepare for the next one and we want to develop winners here, as those guys are all aware. There are times I don't want to see the players and they will go in and keep things alive, keep an energy around the place, pick them up and we will come in at the end of the week."

It was fitting that the championship finale would take place at the same ground where the manager had been on the brink of resigning earlier in the season. In mid-October, a stuttering Celtic had trailed Kilmarnock by three goals at half-time. Already a considerable distance behind Rangers in the SPL, it was an intolerable situation. Had events not improved after the interval, the Hoops boss would have considered his future. He had to deliver the most important team-talk of his life. It had the required result. Celtic managed a miraculous recovery and secured a point. From that point on, they never looked back.

"Football is unpredictable," he said. "You have to keep going until the final whistle, until there is no more left, but I did feel that day at Rugby Park that if it got any worse I would seriously consider my position. I was never under pressure from Peter Lawwell, Dermot Desmond or the board, but it was all about personal pride.

"Where was I going with this team? Where was I taking it? However,

I assessed what we did the season before and concluded there couldn't be a lot wrong. It was more a confidence thing. True enough, we won at Motherwell then picked up a couple of good results in Europe and our confidence grew. To come back to Rugby Park and be eighteen points clear was great. But I was worried it might have been too late."

The contrast in emotions during the interval in both games couldn't have been starker. This time Celtic had raced into a 4-0 advantage following a scintillating first-half display. They added a further two goals without reply after the break. It had been a dazzling display of attacking football – a display worthy of champions. That fact made it all the more enjoyable.

"I looked back on it with huge pride," said the manager. "It was just a great day for the club as a whole, whether it be myself and the back-room staff, the players, the board and the supporters. It was a perfect day in terms of how we want to play football and for how we want our support to sing for us and follow us. Ultimately, we had brought the championship home. It had been a while since we had it but now we could say we were the champions and it was a fantastic feeling."

At times, particularly when Celtic's form fluctuated in the first part of the season, some questioned whether the players were capable of embarking on a title triumph. Not Neil Lennon. There was a strong camaraderie and unity between the squad and the management team. It was a powerful weapon.

"I had felt it for a long time," said the manager. "I couldn't have asked for a better bunch of players to have worked with. I was very proud of them. I had a great captain in Scott Brown. We had a great dressing room. On the Wednesday before the Kilmarnock game, we took them all out for a meal and that's something we didn't often get the opportunity to do.

"We had a private room, had a bit of dinner and watched the football. There was a great spirit and great togetherness and I think that relaxed them going into the game. Every now and again, it's good to do that for the team and the backroom staff as well, but there's a healthy respect between the backroom staff and players and you can see that it magnified itself during the game."

When Celtic crossed the winning post, the gap between themselves and the remainder of the SPL was a massive twenty-one points. They had clinched the title in devastating fashion in Ayrshire. By any measure, Celtic thoroughly deserved to be champions. In February, Rangers had been docked ten points for entering administration.

Simple arithmetic showed that this sanction had no impact on the final outcome of the championship, yet some supporters from the blue half of Glasgow used this to claim Celtic's championship to be 'tainted.' This was as predictable as it was ludicrous. What was more surprising was that a small number of pundits within the mainstream media also decided to spout this absurd view. Celtic's hefty points tally and their statistical supremacy made a mockery of that argument. No wonder it irked Neil Lennon.

"It was an accusation thrown at us from people in the game," he said. "I don't mind it coming from supporters on the other side but when it comes from people who have actually played the game it really disappoints me. Like all sports, if you win something and you've cheated then it's tainted. We hadn't done anything wrong as a club and the players hadn't done anything wrong on the pitch. They had played the best football, scored the most goals, conceded fewer than anyone else, and have played the best football, so they were worthy winners. We also had the best disciplinary record, so not only were we respecting referees, we were respecting our opponents and respecting the game. It was only people who were sore losers who were trying to come out with these small gripes and digs, and that meant nothing to us really."

Celtic had already overtaken Rangers and were accelerating away from them at the SPL summit by the time the Ibrox side suffered their points penalty. It only hastened the inevitable.

"Rangers didn't go into administration until six weeks after we had gone top of the league, and by that time we were like a juggernaut going through the league," said the Hoops boss. "The swing was with us, the football was with us. We just looked like a team who would be difficult to stop. We were still in all the cup competitions as well and I think sometimes the amount of games the boys play gets overlooked. I don't know how many we have played this year but I'm sure it would be well into the fifties. Most neutrals even say we were the best footballing team, and it was good for the game up here that we had won the title."

THE champagne had been on ice for a while. Having accrued such a handsome advantage over their rivals in the SPL, it was only a matter of time until Celtic were crowned champions. This was certainly preferable to being involved in a closely-contested battle for the title and all the subsequent pressures, but it wasn't without its difficulties. With the finishing line in sight, and no challengers in close pursuit, maintaining a resolute mindset can become tricky. If mental fortitude dips even slightly, it can cause a downturn in displays, making the final stride across the line a slog rather than a canter.

Throughout their twenty-match winning run in domestic football, Celtic had successfully followed the mantra of focusing on each game in turn to avoid this dilemma, much to the frustration of the media who were offered the same 'one game at a time' answers at press conferences.

Of course, Celtic's sole concern was not on creating interesting copy for the Scottish media but winning matches and it was a formula that had been working. A 3-2 away defeat to Rangers in March had been the Hoops' only league defeat since October. It also denied them their first chance of being confirmed champions, compounding the disappointment. The Bhoys had got back on track with a hard-fought home victory over a stubborn St Johnstone and that presented them with a second chance for a title celebration at Rugby Park. With six games remaining, they only required a draw against Kilmarnock to lift the trophy. The anticipation was building among players and fans.

"We could almost touch it," said the manager. "The players had been fantastic all season and they knew they just had a bit of work to do. I thought they would be a bit more relaxed. They had done the majority of the hard work and they just had to play one game – we hoped we could finish it off with a bit of style.

"I felt there was more anticipation in terms of looking forward to the game. We were bringing a huge following and that benefited the players no end. It was just a matter of keeping the anticipation tempered. Preparation was no different to any other week and I thought the players were looking forward to it. Obviously, we had to win it first or at least get the point to win the title. But you remember these days for the rest of your life."

Almost exactly five years earlier, Celtic were in a similar position ahead of a game away to Kilmarnock. Boasting an enormous lead in the league, Gordon Strachan's side only required three points to seal the championship. It was a day which had a dramatic ending. Deep into added time, a sublime free-kick from Shunsuke Nakamura flew into the far corner, sparking scenes of delirium. Neil Lennon was the team captain that day. He remembered it vividly.

"We were in a similar position to where we were before the Kilmarnock game," he said. "We were miles clear and were just lacking a bit of intensity going into a few of the games and we scratched our way over the line. It was set up beautifully for Naka to score the winner in the last minute, so cue the celebrations and the release, the culmination of a year's work coming to fruition. The celebrations afterwards were fantastic.

"I would've taken anything, so long as we were champions by the end of the day. The sooner we did that the better for everyone associated with the club, in particular the players and supporters."

Like that game in 2007, these are memorable events which are never forgotten. This was a chance for the players to strike their name into club history.

"Allied to the Celtic-Rangers games, these are the ones the fans remember the most," explained the manager. "You look back over the years at title-clinching victories such as the one where Celtic went to St Mirren and won 5-0 while Hearts got beat that day. Fans remember that for the rest of their lives and the players could etch their own names in the club's history by achieving something at Rugby Park."

They certainly did that. Celtic were determined, relentless and ruthless. The hosts were swept aside and had no answer. Within the first ten minutes, the fate of the title had, in effect, already been decided as the Hoops stormed into a two-goal advantage. Charlie Mulgrew, outstanding throughout the season, was the inspiration. He was an unstoppable force.

"Charlie had been brilliant," said the Irishman. "He came on a free transfer from Aberdeen but we knew he had certain qualities that would make us better. He took time to adjust but once he found his feet he was so consistent and he signed off the championship with a performance of great beauty. Everything you could ask of him he had done that day and it encapsulated his season."

Mulgrew, who would also win his first Scotland cap in the course of the 2011/12 season, opened the scoring with a header from Ki Sung Yueng's corner and then turned provider for the second goal, delivering a wonderful cross for Glenn Loovens to convert at the far post. It had been a whirlwind start. In the 36th minute, Mulgrew added his second in spectacular style. After another foraging run forward from left-back, he cut inside the box and curled a superb right-foot shot into the far corner.

Cammy Bell managed to deny Georgios Samaras but there was still time for a rampant Celtic to add a fourth before half-time. Again Mulgrew was involved, sending another terrific delivery into the box which Gary Hooper volleyed into the net. With such a commanding lead, the game was effectively over. Although Kilmarnock improved after the break, Celtic also had chances to add to their tally. Loovens was unfortunate in being unable to finish off a sweeping counter-attack. In the closing minutes, Celtic finished with a flourish. Substitute Filip Twardzik, making his third appearance for the club, flicked a return pass through for Joe Ledley who chipped the ball over the advancing Bell. Hooper then rounded off a perfect performance with a rasping half-volley from the edge of the box. Attractive, entertaining and combined with a fierce will to win, Celtic had been unstoppable. No barrier would have halted their progress in this form.

"It epitomised the season, not just this season but the two seasons," said the manager. "We had played some wonderful, free-flowing football and it was there for all to see at Rugby Park. We were in the mood and it would have taken a very good team to have stopped us. The mental strength was there, allied to the great ability the players all had. As a team it just all came together on that particular day. It was exciting, fast, young, energetic and full of quality. In the previous couple of weeks we had looked a bit mentally tired but the win over St Johnstone set us up for the game at Kilmarnock.

"Everyone came to party, but the players still had to go out to perform, and they did that in emphatic fashion. I was so pleased we had done it in the style we did. It was breathtaking. They're vibrant, they're young and they're naive at times, but you had to understand that with young players – but what an achievement. We had eight out injured and Victor suspended so we had nine players missing. We had a couple of kids on the bench, which was great. Young Twardzik came on and I thought he had a fabulous second half. They are talented players, and sometimes with them being young they tail off a little bit, and I understood that, but to do this with a squad as young as this filled me with even more pride."

Just three weeks earlier, Kilmarnock had stunned Celtic in the League Cup final, ending the treble dream. Evidently, the pain of losing at Hampden had fuelled a desire for revenge.

"It was a bit of karma after the League Cup final," said the manager. "We did to Kilmarnock that day what we should have done to them in the final. We absolutely murdered them. In terms of opportunites in the League Cup final, we missed easy chances that day, and as a manager there is not a lot you can do about that. It just wasn't our day."

Following the recent reversals to Kilmarnock and Rangers, had Celtic failed to take the spoils at Rugby Park, questions may have been asked over the Hoops' ability to cross the finishing line. Their response had been emphatic.

"We'd had a lot of good performances like that over the whole season and sometimes it got a little bit lost," said the manager. "We had been on a brilliant run but lost the cup final and then also got beat by Rangers. Suddenly everyone thought we had become a bad team again, which is obviously nonsense. The players answered the undue criticism that was coming and they won the title in emphatic fashion."

As the final whistle sounded, months of tensions were released. Neil Lennon exchanged handshakes with his counterparts from Kilmarnock before embracing Johan Mjallby and the rest of the coaching staff. Visibly emotional, he strode on to the pitch to celebrate with his players and receive the adulation of the travelling support.

There was no trophy to grasp – that would need to wait for another day – but it didn't detract from the euphoria or joy. These were scenes to treasure. After a mass huddle, the players and backroom staff embarked on a lap of honour around the ground which was a sea of green and white, along with the odd inflatable champagne bottle, on three sides. Kilmarnock had handed over an extra stand to accommodate the incredible demand for tickets from Celtic fans determined to be present for the title party. Around fourteen thousand of them had crammed into the ground, creating a deafening noise during the game. It was an unforgettable atmosphere.

"I couldn't thank the supporters enough," said the manager. "It was like a home game. It was like one of those special days that you tend to forget when you're a manager and have played. We had some great days and they all came flooding back. You could see what it meant to players. They really appreciated the support and the connection between the players and fans is there now. The club is united again and that is very special.

"You could see it in the supporters at the end. They have always had the pride in the club but you could just see it bursting out of them and their affection for the players. For me, that was very important when I took the job on, to get the supporters back on side again and get the connection between everyone at the club again. When it's like that, the feel-good factor is fantastic and the club gets on a roll. We wanted to build on that."

Up at Celtic Park, supporters had started to congregate even before the final whistle had sounded at Rugby Park. By the time the team bus arrived back in the East End of Glasgow from Ayrshire around four thousand jubilant fans had surrounded the entrance to the stadium. As the players appeared at the front door of Celtic Park, a deafening roar broke out.

"They understood it then, if they didn't get it before," said the Hoops boss. "I'm sure they got up on the next morning feeling great and maybe with a sore head but feeling great, and they were entitled to do that as they had worked very hard and been through some tough times. But what they had showed was staying power, which is very important to be a championship team. They had brushed away the disappointments and come again and were in a good place. They should hold on to that feeling they had as it might never come again in their careers, but they now knew how it feels to be a champion at this club – and it's pretty good."

Even as the party was in full swing, Neil Lennon was already contemplating the future. Another challenge always lies on the horizon for a Celtic manager and he was already planning on how to build on this success. There were reasons to be optimistic, particularly from the youthful make-up of the side which took to the field at Rugby Park. At the age of twenty-eight, Kris Commons was the oldest player on the pitch, with the vast majority of the side still in their early twenties. Greater experience would only bring improvement.

"Not only have they got the talent but they have great temperaments as well. It's a young side and we're building something we think is special. I look back to what I was doing when I was the same age as the likes of Adam Matthews and James Forrest. I was at Crewe in front of maybe three or four thousand people, under no pressure. These guys were doing it front of sixty thousand every other week, with huge expectations.

"Ultimately, my remit was to come in and win the championship and I feel great we have done that and built this team which will hopefully stand this club in good stead for the next couple of years. We want to add to it, obviously. We want to try and find extra quality in certain areas and take the team on. We built a young, vibrant squad from the remnants of 2010 and came very close last year, which was a nice surprise because we were so far behind the year before. There was a real motivation to go one better this year, though, and they had done it in spectacular fashion."

Hampden
Heartache

NEIL LENNON has an insatiable appetite for silverware. While the league championship was the prize that took precedence, he was also in the hunt for both domestic cups. The failure to land the Scottish and League cups when they were within his grasp remains painful. At one stage, an historic treble seemed a real possibility. Cantering towards the title, the Hoops faced Kilmarnock in the League Cup final. They were overwhelming favourites but couldn't find a way past an inspired Cammy Bell in goal for the Rugby Park side. In the closing minutes, they were punished as Dieter Van Tornhout headed in a late winner. It was desperately disappointing. The treble dream was over.

However, the gloom quickly lifted as Celtic sealed the title in sparkling style. Attention then turned towards the task of retaining the Scottish Cup. Just Hearts stood between the Hoops and a place in the final, the perfect culmination to a memorable season.

Celtic dominated the first half of the match without reward. As the tension grew, the Tynecastle side drew first blood when Rudi Skacel fired them into the lead. Gary Hooper's late leveller looked to have sent the match into extra-time but, with seconds to spare, Hearts were awarded a controversial penalty. It was a huge decision. Former Celt, Craig Beattie, converted from the spot. Another trophy had gone. A burning sense of injustice over the award of the penalty made it all the more difficult to swallow. With the championship already secured, the season was effectively at an end.

Celtic's unexpected defeats sparked an inquest: Why had they been beaten by these teams when so much was at stake? Did they lack the ability to deliver on the big stage? In the immediate aftermath, the manager launched a passionate defence of his players – they had the better of both games, they had created enough chances to win, they had turned up. Fate had simply conspired against Celtic on both occasions. Given the opportunity to pause and reflect, his opinion hasn't changed. Not that it diminished the disappointment.

"The season was over," he said. "We were out of the competitions. The semi-final is still a bit raw but I look at both the games – the League Cup final and the Scottish Cup semi-final – and ask myself, 'Did we play well?' I think we did. Did we dominate the games? Yes, we did. Did we create really good chances? We missed simple chances in both games to put the teams away. That happens in football. A couple of decisions went against us at crucial times, and that's the beauty of cup competitions – sometimes lady luck isn't on your side. But for it to happen a second time was hard to take.

"It's a different environment – don't get me wrong, it's the same for both teams. The pitch is a bit slower and the ball is different from what we are used to in the league competitions but I wouldn't use those as excuses. Anyway, we won two semi-finals last year so it's not really a productive argument. I look at the performances in both matches and we have played worse and won. So I can't be over-critical of the players. The only criticism I would have is that when the chances come along – take them.

"If you're creating chances and forcing the goalkeeper to make saves, passing the ball and keeping possession for long periods and teams are just hanging on to your coat-tails and you aren't putting them away, then there is always a chance they might get a break and score. That's basically what has happened."

Football can be a cruel game at times. It was all the more galling given the extent of Celtic's efforts in the competitions. The road to Hampden had been long and demanding. In every round, the Hoops faced tough away ties, travelling to the furthest corners of the country, enduring all manner of testing conditions. It had all been in vain. There was nothing tangible to show for it in the trophy room at Paradise, and that is what clubs like Celtic are, ultimately, judged on, a reality not lost on Neil Lennon. However, concentrating on the two matches where the dreams evaporated would paint an incomplete picture of Celtic's cup exploits. You must rewind to the very beginning – to a torrential autumn night in the Highlands.

WHEN Celtic were drawn away to Ross County in the fourth round of the League Cup, it was not just a difficult fixture against a team riding high in the First Division, it was a rematch of the 2010 Scottish Cup semi-final where the Hoops had infamously lost in one of the biggest cup shocks of recent memory. Naturally, this heightened interest and was a major pre-match talking point.

The defeat was certainly not something Neil Lennon wished to recall but, irritatingly, there wasn't much choice. He knew the only way he could banish discussion of that match was through a victory in Dingwall. That was his full focus. Furthermore, Celtic had been the beaten finalists the previous season in the competition. He was anxious to redeem that loss.

"Ross County had beaten us in the semi-final a couple of years beforehand," said the manager, "but we weren't thinking about that. We were going to be positive. It was a cup competition which we wanted to get to the final of, like we did last season, and we went there with the right frame of mind. They still had some players who had reached the final, and obviously they still had Derek Adams there as manager, who had them well-organised. It was a difficult game. Any away game, even to a First Division team, can be filled with danger, so we just had to be careful."

Everything seemed to indicate an upset before kick-off − Celtic's variable form at that juncture in the season, the dreadful weather conditions and the confidence of the home side. However, the Hoops prevailed, and deservedly so. Gary Hooper's first-half strike and a Scott Boyd own goal after the break ensured Celtic's progress to the next round. The shock on the night didn't occur at Victoria Park but at Falkirk as Rangers, who had beaten Celtic the previous weekend, exited at the first hurdle to their lower-league opponents.

"On the back of the defeat at Ibrox, people might have been thinking we were a bit vulnerable so I was pleased," said the manager. "It was difficult and you are always looking to see what character the players had and they showed that."

Celtic's reward was an away day in the capital against Hibernian, who had seen off Motherwell on penalties in the previous round. A win at Easter Road would book the Bhoys a place at Hampden in one of January's semi-finals. The Hoops had yet to hit top form in the league but there had been signs that they were beginning to click into gear. Maintaining that momentum was vital, as was reaching the last four of the competition. It was a match of huge significance.

"It was a very important game," said the Irishman. "It was a game we wanted to win to build some momentum going into the following weekend as well. We tried to pick the strongest possible team because it was a cup competition we wanted to win. It was just important to win the games and we wanted to be challenging in all competitions. We got to the final the previous season and we wanted to go one better this year. It was a very big game, as all the games coming up would be. We had had a decent few games if you considered the comeback against Kilmarnock, the good performance against Rennes and a good win the weekend before. So considering the amount of players who were out, we were holding up okay."

Just five minutes into the match, Celtic found themselves behind as Ivan Sproule's driven cross-shot was deflected into the net off Daniel Majstorovic. Anthony Stokes struck the post for the Hoops but, in truth, it was a below-par first-half display from the visitors.

"That was down to us losing possession in bad areas and losing our positional discipline," reflected the Hoops boss. "We had been in the final third attacking and our decision-making on the ball was poor. When you do that, you leave yourself open to any counter-attacks. We had a chat with them at half-time about passing the ball properly in the right areas and everyone saw the results from that."

It was a different tale after the restart as Celtic were transformed. James Forrest levelled the match with a fine run and strike into the far corner just a minute into the half. The youngster was simply unstoppable and he doubled his tally after collecting a return pass from Stokes and finishing with aplomb. Stokes headed home number three from a corner, before Hooper completed the scoring for a dominant Celtic, latching on to Adam Matthews' long ball and sweeping a shot beyond Mark Brown in the Hibs goal. In the end, it was an emphatic victory. Celtic were on their way to Hampden.

"I was pleased to be into the semi-final as we could put that to bed for a couple of months and concentrate on the league, but it gave the players something to look forward to. There was a semi-final at stake and I didn't want to end that run going in all competitions. It could have done on the first-half performance, but the second-half performance was magnificent.

"In the second half we were absolutely exhilarating. It was as good as we had played for a while and the sort of performance we had been asking from them. When they put it all together and play as well as that as a team, they are really good to watch and easy on the eye. The players had shown plenty of character, and I was so pleased with them because it had been such a big game."

Celtic's opponents in the last four were the conquerors of Rangers in the fourth round: Falkirk. Managed by former Celt, Steven Pressley, the Bairns had put their faith in youth, filling their side with players from their Academy, with impressive results in both the league and cup. Along with the Ibrox side, they had also taken the notable scalp of Dundee United in the competition.

"Falkirk had been excellent this season," said the manager. "You looked at that sort of run and you thought their name might be on the cup. They had had two terrific results, beating Rangers, who were in good form at the time, and then going away to Dundee United and winning on penalties was fantastic. They had also been pretty consistent in the league. They were a young team but played with no fear. I was sure that would be the case on the day at Hampden."

Despite this, Celtic, on the back of thirteen successive victories, were still expected to prevail with some comfort. The manager held a more cautious outlook. As someone with considerable semi-final experience, he knew they were significant obstacles to negotiate, regardless of the level of opposition. The reversal to Ross County was a stark reminder.

"Semi-finals are very difficult games," he explained. "We know they are fraught occasions and it's all on the day. If you don't prepare properly you could be in for a fall. Looking at the season, if you could get to the final, you could put it to the back-burner and then have something to look forward to. But we knew we had maybe ninety minutes, or even one hundred and twenty minutes and penalties in front of us. We didn't want to make the same mistake we made against Ross County. It showed the dangers that are there if you took your eye off the ball. From our own point of view, we were in three competitions and we had got to the final of this one last year. We fell short in the final and the players wanted to get another crack at the final."

After a frenzied opening to the game, Celtic gradually stamped their authority on proceedings and began to fashion some decent opportunities. Scott Brown's shot was touched on to the post by Falkirk shot-stopper, Michael McGovern, and Hooper netted from the rebound. The goal was incorrectly ruled out for offside, however. Thomas Rogne then hit the bar with a header from a corner, and he was involved again as the Hoops opened their account. The defender was hauled back by Darren Dods in the box and a penalty was the outcome. Brown sent McGovern the wrong way from the spot. That didn't spell the end of the Bairns' resistance, however, as they spiritedly fought back to restore parity before the break. Kallum Higginbotham picked out Jay Fulton inside the box, and he finished under Fraser Forster.

Rogne, a real threat at set-pieces, headed on to the frame of the goal again in the second half as Celtic looked to restore their advantage. In the 56th minute, they won a free-kick on the edge of the box. Stokes stepped up and dispatched a curling shot into the top corner. As the clock ticked down, the Irishman added his second of the afternoon to condemn his former club to a cup exit, converting from Hooper's cut-back. Just as the manager had predicted, it had been a fight. Nonetheless, Celtic were through to the first major final of the season.

"I was delighted," said the manager. "It was all about the players. They were doing fantastically well. I'm not going to be disrespectful to Falkirk. I thought they made a great contribution to the game, and it was a good semi-final, as semi-finals go. I was just so pleased and proud of my players. They kept getting asked questions and answering them.

"I think in these semi-finals, they are difficult because, one, they are a semi-final and two, this isn't being critical of Hampden, but it's such a vast stadium and sometimes when you have 15-20,000 empty seats it does lack atmosphere. However, I was only concentrating on what happened on the pitch and some of our play was good.

"I thought we dominated the game, particularly in the second half. Falkirk played well but we had hit the bar twice, hit the post, Forrest had a one-on-one and missed, Commons had a one-on-one at the end and missed and Rogne also had a free header at the far post from four or five yards out and missed that. In terms of chances in the game, we had been well on top. I had to rely on my goalkeeper to make a double save at 2-1 in the second half but apart from that I thought we controlled the majority of the game."

All that mattered was the final outcome. Celtic were now one step away from lifting the League Cup, and securing the first piece of silverware of the season was a major objective for everyone at the club. It was also the first trophy that the manager won as a Celtic player and, accordingly, it held special meaning to him.

"It had been a very significant trophy in my career," he said. "It was a trophy that was there to be won. It was a huge day out for the fans and was just as big for the players. It was all about this cup final. It was a trophy that was important to win. It was important to me and important to the players. For some of them, it was their first chance of winning a medal in their careers."

Celtic had reached the same stage the season before, only to lose agonisingly 2-1 to Rangers in extra-time. That memory remained raw for many of the players and the manager. Redemption offered even further incentive.

"I could use a lot of games to motivate the players, none more so that the cup final last year," explained the Irishman "Some of the players didn't do themselves justice that day but they had the opportunity, which doesn't come around that often, to rectify where they went wrong. I thought that would be a motivation in itself but we also had our own reasons for wanting to win the cup."

Kilmarnock stood in the way of that aim, and no-one at the club was complacent about their threat. Celtic had witnessed that at first hand in the 3-3 draw in October.

"They had done very well," said the Hoops boss. "They had probably tailed off a little bit in terms of the top six but it was a cup final and anything could happen on the day. We had to keep that excitement tempered because it was just a game of football we had to win, regardless of the occasion. We had lost in the final last year so I was sure the players would be pretty motivated to go one better. We just tried to balance the excitement with the reality of the fact it was just one more game they had to win."

With that objective in mind, Celtic made a purposeful start. A poor pass from Mahamadou Sissoko allowed Hooper to bear down on Cammy Bell, but the normally clinical striker was denied by the onrushing keeper. He also kept out a header from Stokes and a ferocious shot from Brown from twenty yards. At the other end, Forster pushed a shot from Dean Shiels away, before Stokes hacked a header from Sissoko off the line as belief grew among the Ayrshire outfit.

Shiels spurned another chance for the Rugby Park side at the start of the second half before Ledley dragged a shot wide when well positioned. However, it was Bell who continued to be Celtic's main nemesis, saving well from Stokes and Victor Wanyama and then racing off his line to thwart Charlie Mulgrew. The tension was growing. But, with extra-time looming, Kilmarnock broke clear and struck a fatal blow. Lee Johnson scampered down the left and his deep cross was converted at the far post by Dieter Van Tornhout. It was the Belgian's first goal for Kilmarnock.

Celtic pressed desperately for the equaliser but found Bell an impregnable barrier. Samaras saw a volley blocked by the shot-stopper and he also reacted rapidly to save the rebound from Commons. In a controversial conclusion, Stokes was felled by Michael Nelson as he prepared to pull the trigger inside the box. It looked like a penalty. Instead, the referee booked the incredulous striker for diving. It was the last act of a gripping final. Celtic were dejected and disconsolate. The treble dream was over.

"The standard the players had set meant there was huge disappoint-ment that we weren't going to win the treble," admitted the manager. "Those were the standards they had set, so they had made huge strides since we took over. To say we were disappointed, however, was an understatement. We came very close to the treble last year and even closer this year. But we'll try to go one better next year."

The manager couldn't criticise his charges on their display, pointing to the heroics of Bell as evidence of their superiority. It had been one of those days. Not that it provided a crumb of comfort.

"I'm not saying we didn't play well, because we did," he said. "Their goalkeeper got man of the match, so that's indicative of the way we played. Gary Hooper had an early chance and missed — it was a sitter. You would have put your house on it. Then to be fair to Cammy Bell, he made a wonder save from an Anthony Stokes header and tipped one over the bar from Brown.

"Stokesy had a great chance when he cut inside and hit it straight at the keeper. We deserved better. We missed some really easy chances and dominated the second half in terms of possession and chances.

Maybe our name wasn't on the cup. If we had got one, we might have gone on to win the game comfortably. If you don't take your chances in any game of football, you always leave yourself liable to a team nicking a goal, which is exactly what's happened. Then Bell made a double save from Samaras and Commons. Some days your name is not on the trophy. That's football."

The failure to earn a penalty in the closing minutes was still a source of frustration.

"It was a penalty and a sending off at a big moment in the game," added the manager. "I'm not saying we would've scored the penalty, but I think the referee got that one wrong."

It had been a day of immense disappointment but an incident after the final whistle put events in perspective. As Kilmarnock were celebrating their historic victory, Jack Kelly, the father of midfielder, Liam Kelly, suffered a heart attack in the main stand at Hampden.

After being treated by paramedics at the ground he was taken to hospital where he tragically died. Celtic had a lost a cup final. Liam had lost his dad.

"I was there that day in the tunnel speaking to the lad and it was one of those horrible, horrible moments," said the Hoops boss. "I was at the funeral of his father and it was a beautiful service, and Liam had conducted himself with great dignity. To lose any member of your family, but to lose them in such public surroundings can only compound the difficulties and pain you go through, so I think Liam and his family handled the whole situation very well."

THERE are very few clubs in Scottish football that Celtic haven't faced in their 125-year history – but Peterhead was one of them until the start of January. The traditional fishing town on the North East coast was the unusual starting point for the Hoops' Scottish Cup journey. It seemed to be a complete mismatch. While Celtic topped the SPL, Peterhead were positioned near the foot of the Third Division. Progression to the fifth-round seemed a formality. However, no matter how favourable the odds, no outcome can ever be taken for granted. The Hoops had to remain focused and professional.

"We had been to Berwick the year before and only won 2-0 and that was a difficult enough tie, so we had to be very wary," said the manager. "It's a very special tournament to me, and it was part of the three domestic trophies that we still had a chance of winning.

"We went with a strong squad and weren't complacent. We were not going to take this game lightly. We were the holders of this trophy and we dearly wanted to win it again. The lads had got a taste of winning something the previous season – the majority of them for the first time – so it gave them a bigger incentive to do it again this year. There should have been a gulf in quality but anything can happen on any given day. We had to be ready for that. It wasn't as if we could just turn up, play ninety minutes and then go home. We had to earn the right to play and win the game. This was a huge game in Peterhead's history and their players were very highly motivated to take our scalp, so we had to be very careful."

Peterhead's Balmoor Stadium had never seen such an invasion and was packed to the gunnels, with the home support hoping they would bear witness to an incredible upset. But it was never on the cards as an Anthony Stokes hat-trick booked Celtic's place in the next round.

A well-organised Peterhead had managed to halt the Hoops' advances until the 36th minute when Stokes made the breakthrough, the striker side-footing the ball into the net from a Samaras pass after he had embarked on a surging run towards the byline. The Irishman added his second in fine style, rifling a shot into the far corner from the edge of the box. He then completed his hat-trick in the final ten minutes with another tidy finish.

"Staying in the competition was the main point of the game," said the Hoops boss. "We had to make sure we were in the draw. It was important to keep the momentum going and even though these games are fraught with danger, I thought the players handled it very well. Peterhead made life difficult for us for the first fifteen or twenty minutes but once we settled into the rhythm of the game I thought we were fine, and Cha was a real catalyst for us. He kept breaking down the right-hand side, getting into good positions and opening the game up. That forced Peterhead on to the back foot and then we were able to get Ki, Paddy, Ledley and Brown on the ball. Once we got the first goal, it was pretty comfortable after that."

Although there were six changes to the team which had beaten Dunfermline in the league the previous week, the manager had been true to his word in selecting a strong side and giving the likes of Kelvin Wilson and Emilio Izaguirre valuable game-time following their long injury lay-offs.

"We had nine internationalists playing so regardless of the changes we made, it was still strong and competitive," he added. "I don't see anyone better than the other. I see them as being individuals we can use in different games. I felt Kelvin Wilson and Emilio Izaguirre were both ready and it was good to give Thomas Rogne, James Forrest, Gary Hooper and Adam Matthews a break. For people like Kelvin, Emilio, Paddy, even Lukasz too, it was important.

"It was a big game for them because they hadn't had much football in the weeks leading up to the game. I was delighted with their contributions, as well as the whole team in terms of how they set about things. But for some better finishing, we would have won the game a lot more comfortably."

If you had asked Neil Lennon to select a tie he would have preferred to avoid in the next round, then away to Inverness Caley Thistle would have been high on his list – but that was just the scenario Celtic faced after the draw. Rarely, if ever, had the Hoops enjoyed a comfortable win at the Tulloch Caledonian Stadium, and the Highlanders had history with the Hoops in the competition, having taken their scalp on two occasions – in 2000 and 2003. They were a team the manager admired and was wary of in equal measure.

"Inverness is difficult at any time of year," he said. "It was a cup game and we wanted to progress, but I don't think we could have had a tougher tie than Inverness away. Looking at Inverness last year, they had changed a little bit to the way they played and I thought they played some really good football at times. What Terry and his coaching staff had been doing was plucking these players from England on limited money and getting them to play some really good stuff at times. They have always had a great spirit there and I think it's a club to be admired. The players were focused and very hungry. I knew Terry would have Inverness fired up for the game but we were exactly the same."

In blustery conditions and on a difficult surface, it was Fraser Forster who had to make the first save of note, turning a shot from Nick Ross around the post, before Kris Commons and Gary Hooper were presented with a sight of goal for the Hoops. Both sides had offered enterprise but in the 33rd minute, Celtic broke the deadlock. Samaras capitalised on some hesitant defending by Ross Tokely and fizzed a swerving shot past Jonny Tuffey high into the net. The momentum of the match swung firmly in the visitors' favour.

"We had to rely on Fraser early on to provide a good save from Ross, but I felt we were always dangerous," said the Irishman. "Gary Hooper had got into some good areas on a couple of occasions and was a bit unfortunate, but the goal changed the whole psychology of the game. We were rampant after that and I couldn't see Inverness getting back into the game after we got the goal.

"Georgios' goal was amazing. He got a bit of a break because the ball came off Tokely but after that it was all about his quality and Tuffey found it far too hard to handle. I thought he was great. He led the line brilliantly and he was a real presence in both boxes for us. His play in general, and his movement, was very good. It had been difficult to leave Anthony Stokes out, but looking at the conditions we thought they would suit Georgios better."

After half-time, the Hoops bossed proceedings. Samaras and Joe Ledley were both close to converting the same cross, before the Greek striker was unfortunate as his flick came within inches of finding the net. The second goal finally arrived from the penalty spot when the hardworking Hooper was bundled to the ground inside the box after winning back possession on the byline. Brown again found the net from twelve yards. After that, the result was never in doubt. Celtic were worthy winners and through to the last eight of the tournament.

"It was as good as we had played up in Inverness for a long, long time," said the manager. "I was very proud of the team. It was always a difficult tie going into the game. Inverness were on a good run, but our attitude and the way we approached it was fantastic. We were very professional, very strong. We showed good quality and we got another clean sheet, which I was delighted about as well.

"It was a very competent performance from everyone involved. The most important thing was to get into the next round, and we had done that. The boys who came in – Matthews, Samaras, Commons, Kelvin Wilson – were fantastic, and they added to the quality we had shown over those past few months. Our supporters were also magnificent from start to finish and that gave us a lift."

The fans would be on their travels again later that month as Celtic headed to Tannadice for the quarter-final clash with Dundee United. Not that it should have been a surprise. Over three years had passed since the Hoops had last been drawn at home in a cup clash, when goals from Gary Caldwell and Scott McDonald saw off Queen's Park in a routine win at Paradise.

This promised to be a far more testing encounter. Peter Houston's side had been in terrific form since the turn of the year, posting a number of impressive results, including a thoroughly-deserved win over Rangers in the previous round. If Celtic were going to retain the trophy, they were certainly going to have to do it the hard way.

"Dundee United were playing some excellent football when we faced them in the cup," said the manager. "It was a huge game in the context of the season and one we were really looking forward to. Peter Houston's teams always came on strong in the second half of the season and they had done that again. They were on a fantastic run – I think they had had four or five clean sheets and were scoring goals.

"Again, the draw couldn't have been tougher for us – Dundee United away with the form they were in. But it was a good ground for us, it was a packed house and the players were looking forward to the game. We just had to keep focusing on ourselves. That's what we had done all season and that's what we continued to do."

The high-flying hosts were the more enterprising of the sides in the early stages and Celtic had Forster to thank for keeping the scores level after he produced a magnificent save to thwart Johnny Russell from point-blank range. In the 28th minute, though, there was a game-changing incident. Former Hearts right-back, Robbie Neilson, was given his marching orders for elbowing Samaras in the face during an aerial tussle. It was a reckless act from an experienced operator and he could have little complaint. It allowed Celtic to dictate possession, but only in the second half did they capitalise on their extra man. The opening goal arrived eight minutes after the restart. Stokes drove down the left before picking out Ledley with his cross, who turned the ball home. Samaras then doubled Celtic's advantage in the 71st minute, heading powerfully into the net from Charlie Mulgrew's free-kick.

Stokes somehow missed an open goal from twelve yards but swiftly made amends with a crisp finish into the corner as the Hoops started to uncover gaps in the United rearguard with regularity. As the final whistle approached, Samaras was grounded in the box by Sean Dillon and Brown duly rounded off the scoring from the spot for an emphatic victory. Following a below-par first half, Celtic had responded in some style. Another Hampden date had been booked.

"It was a big month and that was a huge test for us," said the manager. "Dundee United were in great form, keeping clean sheets and scoring a lot of goals, so to come through the tie and into the semi-final relatively unscathed was very pleasing. United were well in the game for long periods and they will count themselves unfortunate, though. I thought we were poor in the first half and United were the better team. That wasn't like us and we had to have words with them at half-time.

"I was very disappointed with our forward play in the first half. We had no cohesion, no hold-up play and I felt United were the hungrier team, so we had to work really hard with the players at half-time to get the response I was looking for. The sending off obviously put us in the ascendancy but Dundee United were well-motivated, very competitive and decent going forward. One thing we have is character and the players showed all that, along with their quality in the second half. I think Dundee United tired as they put a lot into it, and obviously they were playing for a long time with the man down, but some of our forward play in the second half was sensational.

"The younger lads really came to the fore at Tannadice. Forrest was brilliant, along with Wanyama, Rogne and Adam Matthews. They had been so consistent this season so that was testament to their mental strength more than anything else."

Celtic's route to Hampden had been littered with considerable obstacles. It would be no different in the semi-final with Hearts providing the opposition. The Hoops were on a high, however, following the resounding 6-0 win over Kilmarnock the previous weekend, a result which had clinched the championship. It had been a wonderful day at Rugby Park in every sense. Now that the players had tasted success at Celtic, it had whetted their appetite for another helping on May 19 when the Scottish Cup final would be decided.

"It had been a great week," said the manager. "The place was vibrant and the players were ecstatic. I didn't think it would take too much to get them back up for the game. The players would have felt immense satisfaction, from what they had achieved. Then you go again. You want more once you have tasted it.

"We had won the Scottish Cup in 2011 and that gave them a taste of success and for me as a manager, you want as many trophies on your CV as possible. We were also going for a fourth domestic final in a row and I thought that was something to incentivise the players. It was the end of the season, the showpiece game, and we wanted to be there."

While the mood was buoyant among the camp, the loss to Kilmarnock in the League Cup final weeks earlier had highlighted how unpredictable these occasions could be. That pain was still vivid.

"I hoped the players would use it as a positive," said the manager. "We had lost the final but there were no recriminations from me as I felt we played pretty well on the day. We had played worse at Hampden and won, so it was a reminder that football is not guaranteed. You had to go out and earn the right to win.

"Hearts were formidable opponents. I had watched them in the previous round, beating St Mirren away. They had good pace in the team and Rudi Skacel and Craig Beattie were a threat. They had good goalscorers as well."

The first half at Hampden belonged to Celtic in terms of possession and chances. Mikael Lustig and Hooper were both off target with headers, while Kris Commons was unable to round Hearts goalkeeper, Jamie MacDonald, after fastening on to a short back-pass. Ki Sung

Yueng was presented with the best opportunity, though, sending a header on to the post from Lustig's delivery. The Hoops were made to pay for those misses just seconds after the restart when Rudi Skacel rounded Forster to put the Tynecastle side in front. Ki fired over and then headed on to the frame of the goal again from Commons' free-kick as Celtic pressed for a swift response. Hearts remained a threat on the counter attack, though, particularly through the pace of ex-Celt, Craig Beattie, who had entered the fray at the break, and Forster was then forced into a smart stop by Skacel's strike from distance.

As the game entered the latter stages, however, Celtic cranked up the pressure, fashioning several opportunities. They were eventually rewarded as Mulgrew's wonderful delivery was headed into the net by Hooper with just three minutes to spare.

The game looked destined for extra-time. But ill-fortune was to strike Celtic at Hampden once again. In the 90th minute, a shot from Marius Zaliukas hit Joe Ledley on the arm from point-blank range. There was nothing the midfielder could have done to evade the flight of the ball. Nonetheless, referee Euan Norris awarded a penalty which Beattie converted. There was just enough time left for Celtic to be denied a similar claim at the other end against Andy Webster. Celtic's last chance of silverware had disappeared. Along with the obvious disappointment, there was a powerful sense of injustice at how it happened. The manager took up his grievances over the decisions with the referee on the pitch after the final whistle. It was an action he later regretted.

"I deeply regret what happened on that day," said the Irishman. "It's the one actionable thing that I did that I shouldn't have. It was an instinctive reaction borne out of frustration more than anything else, but again I know I have to conduct myself better than that."

9

Keeping
The Faith

A NARRATIVE of Neil Lennon's first championship success as Celtic manager should have encompassed purely football matters – the highs, the lows, the turning points. In a normal world that would have been the case, but sadly Scottish football operates in a different, disconcerting sphere at times, something the Irishman alluded to on the day he clinched the title when he described how "things outside of football have affected my life."

From the moment he first kicked a ball in a Celtic shirt over eleven years ago, Neil Lennon has been subjected to a level of vilification unparalleled in the annals of Scottish football. He has endured threats to his life and frequent sectarian and racist abuse, along with direct physical violence. After being appointed Celtic manager, this abuse escalated to frightening levels, culminating in a series of despicable events which continue to make shocking reading. Against this backdrop, delivering the title for Celtic becomes an even more remarkable achievement.

Few would argue that the keen rivalry which exists between opposing teams and their supporters lends the edge that makes the games so vital. Hostility, in varying degrees, from opposition supporters is the status quo at most football grounds. However, the animosity shown to Neil Lennon has been nothing short of astonishing. It was first manifested when he was representing Northern Ireland for the first time since joining Celtic in December 2000. He was subjected to a cacophony of boos by a section of their supporters. This had never been a phenomenon when he had played for Crewe Alexandra and Leicester City prior to his move to Celtic Park. A death threat in 2002, ahead of him captaining Northern Ireland, finally compelled him to quit international football.

At away grounds in Scotland he was consistently jeered, and this notably reached a nasty crescendo whenever he played at Ibrox. Martin O'Neill memorably made a visible show of support to his player after one particular game in Govan where the sectarian abuse and vitriol had reached new levels of hostility.

Some attempted to attribute the behaviour to his reputation as a fierce competitor on the pitch, his robust style, how he would never recoil in the face of adversity. That, they said, made him the natural target for opposition supporters' ire, but it was an argument with feeble foundation. Other players had gained a greater notoriety for their aggressive approach and had collected far more bookings and red cards. Contrary to common consensus, the Irishman's disciplinary record was impressive for a player of his position.

However, the abuse on the pitch was just the prelude to the ordeals he had yet to endure. Verbal taunts soon morphed into direct violence. In 2003, he was attacked by two students in the West End of Glasgow.

The following year, he was the victim of a road rage incident while his daughter was with him in the car. In 2008, while he was first-team coach under Gordon Strachan, he was knocked unconscious in an unprovoked assault whilst on a night out in Glasgow. Both of the perpetrators were subsequently jailed.

Neil Lennon is a strong character, however, and he remained undaunted. In June 2010, he achieved a lifelong dream when he was confirmed as the permanent manager of Celtic, following a temporary spell in charge. This signalled a new wave of abuse and threats. At the start of 2011, he was sent bullets in the post, as were two of the club's Irish players, Paddy McCourt and Niall McGinn. However, events were to take an even more sinister turn. In March 2011, a suspect package addressed to him was intercepted at a Royal Mail sorting office in Saltcoats. A month later, he, along with two high-profile Celtic fans, the late Paul McBride QC and former MSP Trish Godman, were sent what police described at the time as 'viable' devices. This vile act was not the end of the shameful episode.

He was also the target of a repulsive Internet campaign, which led to several people being convicted. For his own safety, he had to be placed under extra protection. A panic alarm was fitted in his home and bodyguards followed his every move. He was placed under round-the-clock surveillance and several security alerts forced his partner and young son to flee their home to a safe house. Now his private life had been completely compromised.

"It was horrible," he said. "You end up putting security measures at your house. I have panic buttons, that sort of stuff. You're driven here, there and everywhere with security people outside your house. I can't thank the security people enough because they've made my life very, very easy under the circumstances. The information we were given was excellent the whole way through. Some of it was very encouraging and some of it was pretty off-putting, to say the least."

The following month, as Celtic took on Hearts at Tynecastle, he was assaulted in the dugout by a member of the home support after the Hoops had scored their third goal of the game. It was a shocking incident which made headlines around the world. Even the sanctuary of the football pitch, his place of work, wasn't safe for him anymore.

All this was happening in the twenty-first century in Scotland. It was scandalous and a stain on Scottish society. Neil Lennon was a football manager. All he wanted to do was get on with his job and his life was being threatened. It had been building up for some time.

"This isn't something that just suddenly happened," he said. "When I joined Celtic as a player I became aware immediately that I was being singled out for special treatment. At first I thought it might just have had something to do with the fact that I was an expensive signing from the English Premiership. That would have been okay, but I became aware of something more sinister when I played for Northern Ireland as a Celtic player for the first time. Before then I had represented my country many times and had enjoyed the full support of the fans. Now I was aware of being jeered by our own supporters every time I touched the ball.

"Then I also began to become aware that I was being jeered at every away ground Celtic played at. Some writers said it was because of my combative style, but I only received two red cards in seven years playing with Celtic and I had never received this treatment while playing in England for three different clubs."

These were intolerable circumstances and the manager prefers to keep his own counsel about how it impacted on his life. It remains a private matter. But he could always rely on the unequivocal support of the Celtic family – backroom staff, players, supporters. Never had the phrase 'You'll Never Walk Alone' seemed so relevant.

"It was difficult and disturbing at times but I had good people around me," said the manager. "The one thing you can do is that you drive up

Victor Wanyama takes the acclaim after powering home a header in a 2-1 win over Dundee United

Anthony Stokes' free-kick puts the Hoops back in front against Falkirk in the Scottish Communities League Cup semi-final

Gary Hooper celebrates scoring Celtic's final goal in the 4-0 rout at Tynecastle (left), while (below) joy for Neil Lennon as Joe Ledley opens the scoring against Dundee United in the Scottish Cup quarter-final victory at Tannadice

A difficult time for Neil Lennon as he acts as a pall bearer at the funeral of close friend, Paul McBride QC, while (right) just 24 hours after the funeral, Neil Lennon leaves the High Court in Glasgow

Victor Wanyama is comforted by Neil Lennon after Kilmarnock shatter Celtic's treble dream in the Scottish Communities League Cup final

(Left) Neil Lennon showing his support for former Celtic team-mate Stiliyan Petrov

(Below) The boss greets his son Gallagher before the home match with St Johnstone in April

Charlie Mulgrew is mobbed by his team-mates after starting the rout at Rugby Park

A proud Neil Lennon soaks up the atmosphere at Rugby Park after becoming a championship-winning manager

The players, backroom staff and supporters celebrate clinching a title which seemed improbable just a few months earlier

(Below) Neil Lennon meets supporters who have gathered outside of Paradise to greet the returning squad

Neil Lennon airs his frustration at referee, Euan Norris, after the controversial conclusion to the Scottish Cup semi-final

(Above) Tony Watt shows the future is bright at Celtic as he drills home his second goal in a dream debut at Fir Park; (below left) Charlie Mulgrew is the centre of the celebrations after opening the scoring against Rangers in April, before (below right) Kris Commons deftly chipped the ball over Allan McGregor to put Celtic 2-0 up

(Above) Smiles all-round as Neil Lennon meets the Thai Tims at Celtic Park

(Left) An emotional Mark Wilson says farewell to Paradise during May's 1-0 win over St Johnstone

(Right) Gary Hooper wheels away after bagging goal number four in a five-star display on title party day

'Don't drop this…', Neil Lennon finally gets his hands on the SPL trophy on the final day

Celebrating on the pitch as the title party gets underway in Paradise

to Lennoxtown, close the gates and get on with your job. The players are a joy to work with and obviously I have had great support from the fans as well."

Somehow, he continued to carry on in the face of these outrages and lead Celtic to a Scottish Cup triumph in May 2011 while narrowly missing out on the SPL title and League Cup. A new season would bring fresh challenges to contend with off the field. It would be a further test of his resolve and character. Thankfully, there would be no repeat of the despicable threats to his life of the previous term but it would still be a testing time, nonetheless.

For a start, there was still the fallout from the previous season. Only a month into the campaign, he was summoned to give evidence in court during the trial of his attacker during the match with Hearts at Tynecastle, describing how it had been "the last straw." The perpetrator, who admitted carrying out the assault, was only found guilty on the lesser charge of breach of the peace, and was jailed for eight months. This would not be Neil Lennon's final court appearance.

In February 2012, two men went on trial for sending the devices in the post which they believed would explode and cause harm to the manager, the late Paul McBride QC and former MSP Trish Godman. Once again the manager had to take leave from his football duties, spend time in the courtroom and explain how his life had been affected. After a five-week trial, the two accused were found guilty of conspiracy to assault Neil Lennon, Paul McBride and Trish Godman and were jailed for five years apiece.

"The court case dragged on for a few weeks and it's not ideal picking up the paper every day and reading about 'Bomb target Lennon'," said the Hoops boss. "At the end of the day, I am a football manager and I have no axe to grind with anyone. It was a little bit disturbing, but Strathclyde Police were fantastic throughout it all, and now that these guys have been found guilty, I'm hoping it will be a deterrent for anyone thinking of doing anything like that again. It's a difficult thing to deal with sometimes. You put on a brave face but sometimes it's very disconcerting. We live as normal a life as we possibly can, but there are restrictions at times in terms of security measures and stuff like that. We're hoping now that spell of intense intimidation – or whatever you want to call it – is over now."

But it wouldn't be in the courtroom where Neil Lennon would endure his most testing time. On Sunday, March 9, Paul McBride QC, a close friend of the manager, was found dead in his hotel room in Pakistan, where he had been on a business trip. He was just forty-seven-years-old. He had died in his sleep of natural causes.

As one of Scotland's most high-profile advocates, and greatest legal minds, the news shocked the whole country. The manager was devastated. Losing someone so close to him, so unexpectedly, was a numbing blow. All the threats, the abuse and the trials, he could handle, but this was difficult to cope with.

"The most difficult time was when we all lost Paul McBride as he was a very close friend of mine and his death was so sudden that it was a real hard one to take. It's still a bit raw with me at times," he explained. "That was the most difficult period, coming to terms with Paul's passing. All the other stuff I could deal with. His death was so untimely and so unexpected and we all miss him. The fact it was so public as well – you would see it every day in the paper. That was just the hardest time as he had done so much for me personally and professionally, and he had done so much for the club as well. He was someone I could turn to for advice, for counsel, for criticism and for humour. He was good that way. He was just a brilliant personality and a huge loss to everyone here in the country, I think."

The day after acting as his pallbearer at an emotional funeral, attended by hundreds of mourners, the manager, in court, described

Paul McBride as the most inspiring person he had encountered in his life, along with Martin O'Neill.

"I had a real difficult time when Paul McBride passed away," he added. "On the Monday it was Paul's funeral and then on the Tuesday I had to go and give evidence in the court case and that was a real tough, tough spell. At times you think, 'Is it worth it?' You know – all these things that happen to you."

In the same month, the manager was also hit with the news that his friend and former team-mate, Stiliyan Petrov, had been diagnosed with acute leukaemia. The announcement stunned the football world and it was particularly distressing for the Irishman, Johan Mjallby and Alan Thompson, who had all played alongside 'Stan' during a memorable era in Paradise. One of the first things they all did after winning the league title was to visit the Bulgarian in a London hospital and show their support for him as he began his battle with the illness, along with passing on the well-wishes of the entire Celtic family.

"Stan rang Roddy Macdonald, our club doctor, on the Friday morning," recalled the manager. "We were training and Roddy pulled us over later. We were close to tears but having seen Stan and spoken with him, seen his spirit and his positivity, we had left him in good form. We talked about football, about Aston Villa and about Celtic. We talked about the years we had under Martin O'Neill and it was all fun.

"We went through a lot of special times together and you forge a bond. Stiliyan was a huge part of the team that got to Seville and had a great couple of years after that before going on to have a great career at Villa. He is part of a very special team that is part of Celtic history. But it is a difficult thing to contend with. It's okay us going to see him but Stiliyan has to go on and deal with this himself and we are very proud of him."

Later that month, the Hoops boss and first-team coach Garry Parker joined Sir Ian Botham during his annual walk for children's leukaemia charities. The Celtic support, meanwhile, made a visible show of their backing for their former hero by holding a minute's applause in the 19th minute of the game against St Johnstone. 'Stan' wouldn't walk alone in his struggle, either. How did Neil Lennon manage to cope amid the turmoil, stress and worry? It was tough, but the secluded setting of Celtic's training complex, at the foot of the Campsie Hills just outside Lennoxtown, provided a sanctuary, where he could fully focus on football – for a few hours at least.

"It's pretty private up there and we can concentrate on our work," he said. "It's a beautiful place – when the weather's nice! But there are great facilities there and once the gate shuts, that's our environment, and where we can get to work without any distractions, so I enjoy that a lot. I could get away by coming up to Lennoxtown where I could close the door and work with the players. That was a reminder of how good life could be."

Aside from the obvious support mechanism of his family, he could also turn to people at the club for assistance and advice, including Dermot Desmond, chief executive Peter Lawwell and members of his backroom team. They were all a great source of strength.

"Peter had been a great support to me as have the board and certainly Mr Desmond as well," said the manager. "My backroom staff have been great and I include John Park and Stevie Woods in that; Roddy Macdonald and Tim Williamson and Kenny McMillan, who has done a brilliant job on our fitness levels. All my staff at Lennoxtown have made life easier for me in terms of the stuff that's been going on outside. Of course, my family has been a great source of comfort to me. I don't want to go down the road of talking too much about it but I couldn't have done the job without them."

When the threats reached their zenith, there were times he contemplated giving up and leaving all the hate behind. No wonder.

"At the end of the day, your personal safety is in jeopardy or you feel it's in jeopardy," he admitted. "I was always well briefed by the police and the intelligence officers, so that gave me a lot of comfort through those times but you're just thinking, 'Is it worth living here?'"

The manager continues to reside in the heart of Glasgow. In spite of everything that's happened, he still loves the city, and the people, and hasn't contemplated of settling in more sedate surroundings.

"I love Glasgow. There are just places I choose not to go to for obvious reasons. I find that a bit sad, that there are places I feel uncomfortable in now, but I can't see myself living anywhere else. I've lived here for twelve years and it's my home. I enjoy the atmosphere of the city. There are things regarding the football side of it I'd like to eradicate. It's easy to say: 'Well, that's Glasgow for you.' It's not. It's not Glasgow. There is more to Glasgow than sectarianism.

"That seems to be what Celtic and Rangers get tarred with, that edge. It's good to have the edge but you have to limit it to the confines of football. When it goes beyond that it becomes a worry.

"I feel like a Glaswegian. I'm entrenched at the club and have lived in the city ever since I arrived. I'm a familiar face to the majority of people of Glasgow. I get well treated by the majority of people in the city and it has been my home. Whether people see me as an honorary Glaswegian, that's another thing – but I feel like one."

That he never yielded in the face of such appalling threats to his life, and trying personal events, is testament to his strength of character and dedication to Celtic. After two torrid years, he emerged triumphantly with the league championship and could look forward to the future with optimism. Neil Lennon doesn't do walking away.

A FACE contorted in rage. The snarling figure on the touchline. Aggressive, uncompromising and argumentative. These are how some view Neil Lennon in Scotland. Those close to him would recognise someone completely different from this public persona – friendly, warm and good company. However, the traditional picture painted of the Celtic manager in some parts of the media leads many to take the former view.

Sure, the Irishman doesn't adopt a serene or laidback demeanour during games. He is a passionate person and possesses a deep desire to win, and he exhibits these emotions during games. It's part of his make-up. He had the same traits as a player. It's something supporters love to witness, and judging by their determined performances on the pitch, it has certainly rubbed off on his players. Many other managers display similar traits in the dugout but Neil Lennon believes he's often castigated as public enemy number one. There is evidence. Ahead of the powder-keg occasion of September's Glasgow derby the *Daily Record* carried the ill-judged headline on the eve of the match: 'WHO'S MORE HATED AT IBROX? (Is it Lennon or the taxman?)

Given the despicable events of the previous season when the Celtic manager was subjected to a campaign of hate, and suffered a physical assault on the touchline at Tynecastle, it was not only inflammatory but highly irresponsible. Following a complaint from the club, the paper published an appropriate retraction and apology the following week. When he reads headlines like that and sees the way he's portrayed in other instances, he can't help but feel he's been demonised.

"That's a fair point to make," he said. "If you had a fair-minded person looking at it, they wouldn't see it any other way. Whatever the idea, it is grossly exaggerated to the point where I'm made out to be public enemy number one. There is a total imbalance in the way the media portrays me, my players and the club. Now, I'm not talking about all the media outlets, I'm talking about certain newspapers and certain pundits. Most Celtic fans will know who we are talking about."

It's an irritation and frustration. No one would enjoy that type of caricature. But he's grown immune to it.

"There is an imbalance and I don't like it but I live with it," he added. "It doesn't affect me and doesn't affect my work. I think it's more a slight on them than anybody else. I try to do my job as professionally as I can."

Neil Lennon will freely admit to having crossed the line of acceptable behaviour during a match on a few occasions, but that's a line that almost every manager has crossed in their time. It happens. Football is an emotional game. The stakes are high and the pressure is great. Towards the end of the season, he hit the headlines for confronting referee Euan Norris on the pitch after the Scottish Cup semi-final defeat to Hearts at Hampden. The Tynecastle side had booked their place in the final, courtesy of a controversial penalty awarded in added time. It was the one action during the season he regretted, and he apologised in the aftermath and accepted his subsequent punishment in the form of a touchline ban.

"It's one actionable thing I had done that I shouldn't have done," he said. "There are the days where I cross the line and I'm taken to task over it but I'm no different to any other manager. I have seen managers do a lot worse than me and it gets laughed off, but when it's me, all hell breaks loose."

He pointed to an example to substantiate his claims. As the English Premier League reached its climax in 2011/12, Manchester City and Manchester United squared off at the Etihad Stadium. Just three points separated the sides in the title race. With three games remaining, it was a match which could help determine the destiny of the title. The pressure was immense and the tension was palpable.

In the closing minutes, as the home side attempted to preserve their fragile one-goal advantage, Sir Alex Ferguson and Roberto Mancini ad a furious verbal spat on the touchline. Both managers had to be kept apart as angry words and gestures were exchanged. The incident was covered yet there was no uproar about their behaviour. Instead, their passion was praised. It was something to savour in an increasingly corporate game. Had Neil Lennon been involved in a similar event in Scotland, would there have been a different reaction? Would there have been a furore? Most certainly, according to the Hoops boss.

"I saw the greatest manager in the game having a spat with Roberto Mancini," he said after that game. "Where I was watching it, people enjoyed it. They enjoyed Sir Alex showing that passion that he was up for the fight. At times we do get lost in the game but if you take that away from us then you are going to have robots on the touchline just sitting with their hands in their pockets, not doing anything.

"I enjoyed it – two managers sticking up for their own team. Was there a huge public outcry over it? No. They talked about a bit of a spat. Big deal. When we do it up here, there are two pages full of it, I get singled out, demonised, and I'm this snarling presence on the touchline. So I don't think I get a fair deal at times. You cannot take away the human element from managers. We are human beings at the end of the day. There are times we get angry. There are times we get aggrieved and there are times when we make mistakes in that aspect of the game, but I think I get a rough ride from it to tell you the truth. Over the course of the season, up until the Scottish Cup semi-final, there wasn't one thing I did wrong. I had the incident at Ibrox which I had the hearing for and then the incident in the semi-final.

"So over the course of the season with the amount of games we played, we are talking about one incident. I don't really think I have to change that much but I will temper those actions if I can. I've seen managers on the pitch remonstrating with referees before, and a lot more experienced than me, but I don't think they get half the rope I get. I just think I should be cut a bit more slack at times."

Given the enduring image of Neil Lennon in Scottish football, that seems uncertain. However, he won't change. His passion for managing Celtic will never diminish and he will continue to show his emotions on the touchline in the seasons to come. Some people will find him objectionable. So be it.

"Listen, this job is a huge privilege for me," he said. "I have always wanted it. I want to be a success in it, for as long as I want to be here really. The passion comes from within – you can't give it to people. Every manager is different. Some are very cool, calm and collected on the sidelines, and some like to vent their emotions and I happen to fall into that bracket as that's just the personality I am. It's not to everybody's taste, but I'm not going to change for that."

That's
Entertainment

THE defensive department can often be overlooked in favour of the more alluring aspects of the game – goals, trickery and entertainment. Football's most feted players are generally masters of the creative arts – Lionel Messi, Maradona, Pele, Cruyff. Wing wizard, Jimmy Johnstone, was the darling of the Hoops support and voted the Greatest Ever Celt. But where would he and the Lisbon Lions have been without the aerial dominance and inspirational leadership of Billy McNeill, the steady presence of John Clark and experience of goalkeeper Ronnie Simpson? Probably not the kings of Europe. They were the rock on which Jock Stein constructed his all-conquering side. Their absence from the team is unimaginable.

The fact is, a mean defence underpins every successful side, and this was certainly true of Celtic in season 2011/12. The Hoops achieved a new SPL record of twenty-five clean sheets over the campaign as they swept to the title. Of the twenty-one goals they conceded during the league campaign, only six occurred at home, the best tally for ninety years, since the days of Willie Maley. These are even greater feats when Celtic's emphasis on attacking football is factored in. Neil Lennon drew significant satisfaction from these impressive statistics at the conclusion of the campaign, and he was keen to highlight them when reflecting on a memorable title triumph. The defence had been the subject of criticism during several stages in the season, and he believed it was an area in the team deserving of praise.

"It was an important foundation," he said. "They are the backbone of the team and it is strong. We have a very good goalkeeper in Fraser Forster, who has been exceptional and he's grown into the role. Then you had the likes of Adam Matthews and Cha on one side, and Charlie Mulgrew on the other, while Daniel Majstorovic had a good spell before he got injured. Kelvin Wilson has been pretty consistent and Thomas Rogne has had a great season. So in terms of this much-maligned defence that keeps getting thrown at us, they have done remarkably well. They also have the best domestic home record of any European league, which again is something to be proud of, so we have built from the back."

Resolute rearguards are normally associated with consistency in selection – the same personnel playing together week after week. The Arsenal back four of the 1990s rhymes off the tongue – Lee Dixon, Tony Adams, Martin Keown and Nigel Winterburn. Their ability to churn out clean sheets became the hallmark of that team as they frequently helped the Gunners to 1-0 victories. It even inspired a song on the terraces. That capacity did not happen overnight. Only by playing together regularly did the players develop the understanding to work as an effective unit.

Neil Lennon was not afforded that luxury, particularly in the first half of the campaign when the defence was decimated by injuries. This started almost as soon as the season got underway. Established left-back, Emilio Izaguirre, suffered a broken ankle in the second league game of the season, against Aberdeen. On the opposite flank, Mark Wilson, who had ended the previous campaign as the first-choice right-back, suffered a recurrence of his knee problem in the autumn, ruling him out for several months. Neither were the club's central defenders immune. Notably, new signing Kelvin Wilson missed over two months with a torn Achilles. At one point, it forced the manager to deploy players out of position and construct makeshift defences on an almost weekly basis.

"It hasn't always been easy to keep a settled back four due to injuries or suspension," he said. "But it just shows that can be a myth at times. You don't need a settled back four to be successful."

Even when the injury situation eased, the Hoops boss rarely enjoyed the opportunity to field the same backline over consecutive fixtures. So how did they manage to maintain such an impressive record?

"They are great pros but what we did was try to keep it fluid so when a player came in, regardless of whether he had been in or out of the team, he knew his job, the team and his position, and he knew what we wanted from him," explained the Hoops boss. "Regardless of whether we changed the whole back four or changed one or two, when they went into the side they knew exactly what their job was."

Hindered by such an horrendous injury list, it was no surprise that Celtic suffered defensive failings in the opening months of the season. The low point occurred at Rugby Park in October as Kilmarnock plundered three goals in a forgettable first half. A combination of injuries and below-par displays damaged confidence, but not irretrievably. The manager pinpointed the visit to Fir Park at the start of November as the turning point for the defence. It was no coincidence that this was the beginning of Celtic's 17-match winning sequence in the league.

"It was the Motherwell game when we started on that great run," he said. "You could just see it in them that day. That there was a determination about them not to get beat and it just sort of blossomed from there. In the two Europa League games in Rennes and Udinese, we were defensively very good against quality opposition, and those performances also gave them a shot in the arm."

The one player who was a constant in the back division throughout the season was Charlie Mulgrew. He stepped into the breach vacated by Izaguirre following his early-season injury and ended the season as an indispensible figure in the team. Whether he operated at left-back or in central defence, he was assured, reliable and also a goal threat at the other end.

"Charlie has been very consistent and has been a good role model for younger players," said the manager. "His quality of play improved as the season went on and he weighed in with eight goals, which is tremendous for a defender. He's a great passer of the ball and for a defender, technically he is very good and has a good football brain. We saw that all manifest itself as the season went on."

When you harvest twenty-five clean sheets over a campaign, there are many defensive highlights to consider. Rather than the occasions where Celtic cantered to victory, it's the matches where a dogged rearguard action was required which stand-out. A tough away day to St Mirren in January typified that sort of performance.

"Rennes away was excellent and we did well with a patched-up back four, and then there was St Mirren away on a really greasy surface and a horrible day," said the manager. "We had to defend very well. St Mirren had a really good spell after half-time and we kept a clean sheet that day, going on to win the game. So games like those, where we had to dig in a little bit and they had to throw their bodies on the line at the time – those performances please you as much as when you win four or five-nil."

In the manager's first full season, a porous defence was transformed into one that achieved twenty-three shut-outs, just two short of 2011/12, which represented rapid progress. However, the manager had identified it as an area of the team which required further strengthening and several new recruits were duly brought in over the summer. Kelvin Wilson and Adam Matthews both arrived on pre-contracts, along with Victor Wanyama, primarily a midfielder but capable of stepping back into a defensive role. Yet, cultivating a strong defensive unit requires two more basic ingredients: mental resolve and hard work.

"There's a mentality to it that you need to work on with the players, and they obviously need to work very hard in training," explained the Irishman. "It takes players a little while to get used to the culture, while the pace of the game is a little bit different and the style of football is a little bit different, too. But overall we have been pretty happy with the contributions they have all made."

Despite breaking records in the past twelve months, the defence will undergo surgery again in the close season. The departures of Mark Wilson and Daniel Majstorovic, along with that of Glenn Loovens and Cha Du-Ri, necessitates the arrival of replacements.

Every good defence requires a good goalkeeper and Neil Lennon believes Celtic possess just that in Fraser Forster. The twenty-four-year-old returned to the club from Newcastle United in August on a second season-long loan spell. His impressive form over the previous twelve months saw the manager designate him as his top transfer target, and the big shot-stopper's displays vindicated the Irishman's determination to bring him back to Paradise.

Forster only missed five of the thirty-eight league games and his consistency between the sticks brought an assurance and calmness to the back division. He also made a critical contribution in a number of matches, making the difference between earning three points or not. Several examples spring to mind – the series of saves he made away to

Udinese, the last-minute penalty save against Hearts in December and the performance against St Mirren in January.

"Fraser has got huge presence, is a very good athlete and his temperament is excellent as well. Nothing seems to faze him," said the Hoops boss. "He enjoys goalkeeping and has been a huge plus for us. He has improved greatly off the back of his first season where we felt he was very consistent. He is only twenty-four, so in terms of goalkeeping that is very, very young. He has got great potential and a great career ahead of him if he keeps doing the right things."

A COMMITMENT to attacking, entertaining football has always been a proud Celtic tradition. From the days of Willie Maley through to Jock Stein, Billy McNeill and Martin O'Neill, it's been a philosophy followed by teams in the Hoops. Neil Lennon adheres to this belief. As a Celtic supporter, and someone who starred in some great goalscoring teams as a player, he understands its importance to the club's ethos.

As a defensively-orientated midfielder, some wondered if the manager would adopt a more pragmatic approach when he was installed in the hot-seat. Not so. He wanted his Celtic teams to be adventurous, exciting and to score goals. He wanted supporters to enjoy watching the team again. His players followed that mantra. In his first season in charge, the Hoops notched up eighty-five league goals in thirty-eight games, producing some sparkling displays along the way, including a record 9-0 trouncing of Aberdeen in Paradise.

Recent trends on the continent suggest a return to prominence of a more defensive doctrine, symbolised by Chelsea's UEFA Champions League success, particularly in the manner they overcame the cavalier Barcelona in the semi-final. However, while the Irishman is at the helm, Celtic will not deviate from their attacking approach.

"It's the only way we want to play," he said. "Now the game might change. If you look at Chelsea and what they have achieved, they have had to play that way against those teams, and I totally understand that. People might look at that now and think we might have to play a little bit more conservatively, but I don't think we can as a club. Our tradition is about playing attacking football and we will try and carry on in the same way."

In the 2011/12 campaign, Celtic fell just one goal short of matching their tally of the previous term. Still, it was a commendable total and they were the highest goalscorers in the league by some distance. Overall, the manager's assessment of the team's attacking performance was overwhelmingly positive. There were some scintillating stand-out showings and some emphatic victories to celebrate.

"The football we played this season has been very good and there were some great performances – St Mirren at home where we won 5-0, Dundee United at home, Hearts and Hibs away, and Kilmarnock away where we won the league. We won those games pretty well and were pretty clinical."

Gary Hooper and Anthony Stokes were responsible for the majority of the goals, while there were also important contributions from the likes of Georgios Samaras, James Forrest, Joe Ledley, Ki Sung Yueng, Charlie Mulgrew and Scott Brown. To have so many members of the side supplying goals was a source of delight, yet the Hoops boss believes there were instances where Celtic lacked a cutting edge.

"There is room for improvement," he added. "If you look at the League Cup final and the Scottish Cup semi-final against Hearts, those were games where we missed easy chances. We do tend to create a lot of chances but I would like to see us improve our conversion rate. But that's me being picky. I'm very pleased with the attacking style of play and with Hooper and Stokes you're guaranteed goals. Sammi has improved this year and the likes of James Forrest, Ki and Joe Ledley, and even Scott Brown to a certain extent, have all weighed in with goals, while Charlie has almost hit double figures, which is impressive from a defender. So from that aspect I'm very pleased. There had been contributions from a variety of players in terms of goals which has been very helpful."

While Samaras didn't offer a plentiful return of goals, he was a major source of supply for others, being extremely unselfish at times when he could have profited himself. For many, the Greek internationalist was an enigma, someone blessed with undoubted talent but lacking the means to produce it on a regular basis. Nonetheless, the manager remained convinced he could put the full package together and was proven correct as the twenty-seven-year-old, frequently deployed in a wide role, emerged as a crucial cog in the attack.

"Georgios was huge for us," he said. "We always knew he had the talent, we just needed to find the consistency, or he needed to find the consistency in his performances. He was a bit hit-and-miss but since he got in the team during the season he was fabulous. He had some brilliant performances. In Italy he was magnificent. When you see him play like that you know he has got it.

"Last season was his best, not in terms of his goal return but certainly his overall performance and what he has brought to the team. He has a great belief in himself, and folk used to wonder if that was misguided, because he wasn't showing that belief in his play. But from October-November time, he was a really big player for us. He has shown tremendous character. It would have been easy for him to say, 'I have had enough here.' He wanted to prove everyone wrong and I have huge admiration for his strength of character."

After his breakthrough season, Forrest became an established presence in the team, consistently terrorising opposition defences with his explosive speed, directness and eye for goal.

"Unfortunately for James, his season was cut short with the injury he got in the League Cup final, but he was tremendous for six or seven months of the season," said the Hoops boss. "He really took games by the scruff of the neck and he's one of those players who gets people off their seats, and is someone we love to have at this football club."

At the outset of the season, an appraisal of Celtic's performance in the final third of the pitch would have been unthinkable without the inclusion of Kris Commons. Signed in the 2011 January transfer window, the creative midfielder hit the ground running for the Hoops, scoring an incredible fourteen goals by the end of the campaign. But, blighted by injury in the opening half of the season, he failed to recapture that kind of goalscoring form, much to the player's own frustration. However, the Scottish internationalist still made a valuable contribution. Despite making just twenty-three league appearances, he provided twelve assists, the highest of any Celtic player. In April, he finally bagged his first goal of the season in the 3-0 victory against Rangers. The manager never lost faith in his ability.

"We had thrown the gauntlet down to Kris before that game and he was terrific for us," he said. "It had been a frustrating season for him in terms of the injuries and probably a lack of confidence on his part, but we always knew we had a good player there and you never lose that ability. It was just a question of working on his mindset. In that month he had been fantastic for us and we were so pleased he got the goal as it really encapsulated his performance."

A predatory presence in the box, someone who has a natural instinct to poach goals, is always a valuable asset to any team. Celtic are fortunate to possess two of them in Hooper and Stokes. The prolific pair found the net on fifty occasions during the campaign. When they failed to hit the heights, there were others who Celtic could depend on.

"It's always handy to have and the two of them have done it well for two years, but like many young players, they can be inconsistent and sometimes we need others to chip and we have that with those players

– James, Joe, Kris, Charlie, Scott and even Victor," said the manager. "So while we have goalscorers predominately in the striking areas, we can score from different areas of the pitch, which pleases me."

Stokes bagged twenty-one goals during the campaign, two better than his total for Celtic in 2010/11. Although he wasn't as prolific in the final weeks of the campaign, the Hoops boss was keen to praise his efforts.

"Anthony's had a great season," Lennon said. "He tailed off a little bit towards the end which, again, is understandable with young players, but I was really happy with his contribution and he can be pretty pleased with his season."

Indeed, the important role performed by Stokes can't be overlooked. Around the months of October and November, when Celtic were low on confidence and fighting to stay in the title race, the Irishman shoul- dered the responsibility and delivered. His goals were important in transforming the Hoops' fortunes.

At Rugby Park, he bagged a brace to help them salvage a point after being three goals down at the break, and he bagged another double to help Celtic beat Rennes and claim their first European win of the season. The striker also struck the leveller against Motherwell as Celtic mounted a comeback to claim a 2-1 win, before another two-goal haul gave the Hoops a crucial win away to Inverness. These were pivotal moments in the season.

"His contribution was huge in those couple of months," said the manager. "I was delighted with him and he should be pleased with himself. He was an important player and we were also trying to prog- ress his all-round game. He was always getting in positions to score goals and is a natural goalscorer, but the rest of his game needed a bit of tidying up and he has been adding to that."

The Irishman enjoyed another productive spell around the turn of the year, which included a hat-trick against Peterhead in the

Scottish Cup and a brace against Falkirk in the League Cup semi-final. In February, he returned to haunt his other former employers once again with a well-taken header in a 5-0 triumph at Easter Road. But it was his overall display which struck the manager.

"That was Anthony's best performance under me," he said. "I couldn't be happier with the way he played – his link-up play, his running off the ball, his unselfishness for the team and obviously he scored a great goal as well. The way he and Gary linked up was top-class. He was a real leader out there. We had been asking for that performance from him and we got it, and he knows now that's his level, so that's all we want from him."

His partner in crime, Hooper, has become one of Scottish football's most feared marksmen since his move from Scunthorpe United in 2010. The striker was a thoroughly deserving recipient of the SPL Golden Boot award, netting twenty-four times, five more than his nearest challenger, Jon Daly of Dundee United. In all competitions, the Englishman bagged twenty-nine goals, seven better than his tally of twenty-two for the previous campaign. Neil Lennon was always confident the hitman had the talent to flourish at Celtic and he expects further improvement from him in the years ahead.

"Gary's a brilliant player, a great goalscorer," said the manager. "He's low maintenance in terms of off the field. He's a very shy and quiet boy but, again, I think there's room for improvement and we have spoken about that with him. But to score twenty-nine goals is a brilliant return. He got twenty-two the previous season so he is averaging around twenty-five goals a season which is tremendous, considering he was relatively unknown when he came in. But we knew how good he was and he will get even better."

After five goals in his first eight matches of the season, Hooper failed to hit the target for five fixtures, a period of the campaign where the entire team were short of self-belief. However, gradually his confidence returned and so did the goals, culminating in a terrific hat-trick against St Mirren in November. After that he never looked back.

"He had injury problems, the team was going through a bit of a crisis of confidence and Gary was just like everyone else," said the manager. "He was a bit off the boil, but we believe in these players and once they found their consistency, Gary showed what a top player he is. Again they can learn from that experience from last season and think, 'I know what it's like to go through a little barren run. I've been there, I've came out the other side and I know I can do it again.'"

Hooper capped off a terrific season with a fabulous five-goal haul in the final game of the season against Hearts on the day Celtic were presented with the SPL trophy. His good form hasn't gone unnoticed, with several clubs down south rumoured to be interesting in acquiring his services. The manager firmly believes he's capable of starring at the highest level, pointing to the example of Nikica Jelavic, who has scored regularly for Everton since his move from Rangers. However, he's anxious to keep hold of his prized striking asset.

"He's a special player and I'm delighted that he's fulfilling all the talent we think he has. He's happy at Celtic. Obviously there will be people out there who would pay for his talent and his goals. He's a goalscorer and they are priceless in the game. But we want to keep him here and will do our very best to do that. If you look at Jelavic and what he's achieved since going to Everton, then there's no reason why Gary Hooper can't do that in any division, whether that be in the Premier League, in Spain or Italy. He scores big goals in big games. He's got a good record against Rangers, he's scored in Europe in the Champions League qualifiers and other European League games.

"He's only twenty-four and has the world at his feet. We would like to keep him. I think he's progressed very well here and I think there's more to come from him in terms of his all-round game but he's in a very good place at the minute."

With the goals of Hooper and Stokes, the searing pace of James Forrest and the skill and versatility of Samaras, the Celtic forward line has the capacity to pose a plethora of problems to any opposition defence. Although the Hoops boss is pleased with the variety of attacking players at his disposal, he's aiming for progression in this department of the team.

"You are always looking to improve," he explained. "Sammi had a brilliant few months when he got into the team. He's not in the team to score an abundance of goals but we would like him to chip in with a few more, but his overall displays were tremendous. Gary and Anthony dovetailed quite well as a partnership and they are always a threat, and we felt James could always score more goals coming into the new season because he's got the ability and the talent. Then, of course, you have Kris Commons in the background. He fed in with one against Rangers but we know he's capable of hitting double figures on a regular basis so there are plenty of attacking options there."

Glittering
Prizes

FOR Charlie Mulgrew and James Forrest this was a season of individual honours. Both scooped a hat-trick of prizes as Scottish football's end-of-season awards were dished out. Mulgrew collected the Player of the Year accolade from his fellow professionals, the Scottish football writers and the SPL. His Celtic team-mate made a clean sweep of the same prizes in the Young Player category. They also came first in the club's awards. These were magnificent achievements and testament to the impact the impressive duo had made over the previous twelve months.

While others experienced fluctuations in form during the campaign, the versatile Mulgrew excelled on a consistent basis, whether positioned at left-back, in central defence or, occasionally, in midfield. He was the stand-out performer in the best team in the country. Forrest, meanwhile, built on the rapid progress of his breakthrough season, establishing himself as an essential member of the side and exciting supporters through his ability to open up defences with his surging runs and acceleration. Naturally, Neil Lennon was thrilled that two of his players had received this level of acclaim, highlighting how instrumental they had been to Celtic's success.

"It's a wee bit of an unknown as you always think that a dark horse might appear but it just shows how well they have played," he said. "James is just an outstanding footballer and is very exciting to watch, very direct and hurts teams whenever he can. He has great quality. Charlie has just improved no end to the point where you can't see him not being in the team. Again, he shows leadership when required and great maturity. He's played some sensational football and to weigh in with eight goals from either centre-half or left-back is a fantastic return."

In the last twenty years, Scottish football's foreign legion have dominated the individual prize-giving, with the likes of Henrik Larsson, Shunsuke Nakamura and Emilio Izaguirre scooping the Player of the Year prizes. In contrast, Mulgrew and Forrest are both Scottish and products of the Celtic Youth Academy who have earned full international recognition. In an era where the standard of the country's football is frequently castigated, the manager believes this is something to be celebrated. Indeed, he paints an extremely upbeat picture of the state of Scottish football.

"There are a lot of good Scottish players around," he explained. "I think there is too much negativity. It far outweighs the positives when people talk about the game up here and that shouldn't be the case because there are a lot of good things about the Scottish game at the minute. If you take away the financial side and the implications and economic side of some clubs, the actual product on the pitch in terms of Scottish players coming through is the best I have seen for a while."

As someone who had always shown great belief in their ability, it was fitting that Neil Lennon shared in their great accomplishments. Plenty of eyebrows were raised when the manager made Mulgrew his first signing upon taking the reins. After all, the defender had previously been deemed surplus to requirements at Paradise. Despite progressing through the ranks at Celtic Park, Mulgrew had failed to figure in Gordon Strachan's first-team plans and was sold to Wolves in 2006 in part exchange for Lee Naylor, seemingly spelling an end to his time at the club he supported.

Hindered by injuries, he failed to make an impression at Molineux and was shipped out on loan to League One side, Southend United, allowing him to finally gain some substantial game-time. After that, his fortunes began to turn. Aberdeen brought him back to the SPL, where his performances and superb set-piece skills caught the eye of Neil Lennon, who took him back to Celtic on the expiry of his contract at Pittodrie. It was an incredible return journey, and affirmed the strength of Mulgrew's character – but it's fair to say that expectations were low from supporters at the first signing of Neil Lennon's reign. After taking a few months to settle, Mulgrew began to vindicate the Irishman's faith in him and prove any doubters wrong. With injuries mounting, the manager handed him a start on the left of midfield in the 2011 Ne'erday clash at Ibrox, and he impressed as the Hoops defied the odds to earn a 2-0 victory over their rivals. It was the spark which lit the fuse.

"Charlie lacked belief when he came back and had a difficult baptism," reflected the Hoops manager. "He was thrown into the Champions League games at left-back and it was a big step up from Aberdeen, but once he found his feet he came knocking on my door one day. He was training well and said, 'Look gaffer, can I get a chance?' I told him, 'You'll get your chance soon.' We played him at Ibrox and since then he has never looked back."

Thereafter, he featured regularly for the rest of that season, predominantly as a central defender, another position he took to with consummate ease. Although he was now an important member of the squad, his stock was set to rise still further. Emilio Izaguirre's injury in the second fixture of the campaign saw Mulgrew moved back out to left-back, demonstrating his valuable versatility once again. As other members of the backline succumbed to periods on the treatment table in those opening months, he remained a constant and commanding presence in the backline. Wherever he was deployed, the performance levels never dipped.

"Charlie looks at home at centre-half, but there were times when he played left-back and was superb," said the manager. "He can play midfield, he can play wide left. He is just a good all-round quality player with a good footballing brain. As long as he is in the team he is happy to play anywhere."

Early in the season when Celtic struggled with consistency and confidence dipped accordingly, Mulgrew emerged as a leader of the side. This fact was acknowledged when he was handed the captaincy in October, and he led from the front at a crucial point in the campaign. In the space of two weeks, he scored a late equaliser against Kilmarnock to rescue a point and supplied Joe Ledley for the leveller away to Rennes, before scoring the winner against former club, Aberdeen, as Celtic clung on in the title race.

"He had been really consistent for us and I was delighted for him," said the manager. "It was the first time he had captained a winning Celtic team. He had played brilliantly for the majority of the season and came up for the winner. It was a credit to him that he went away down south to forge his career and didn't give up on it, and now he was captaining Celtic which was a great achievement for him."

However, tragedy struck the Kirkintilloch Bhoy the following month as his father, Charles Snr, someone who had been a pillar of support throughout his career, passed away at the end of November. It was a difficult time for the twenty-six-year-old, but Mulgrew returned to the side to help Celtic embark on their wonderful winning run and leapfrog Rangers at the SPL summit. After another series of terrific displays in February, which included two stunning goals against Hibs and Dunfermline, Mulgrew was rewarded with his international debut in Scotland's 1-1 draw with Slovenia. It was richly deserved.

"I was delighted for Charlie," said the manager. "He had been fantastic for the best part of eighteen months. He had a tough year personally. He lost his father, but he dealt with that brilliantly. He has a good family behind him and is a credit to the club. Charlie had played very well in the European games so I didn't think international football would faze him. He was one of the most consistent players in the country and he thoroughly justified his selection in the squad."

Mulgrew's progress would continue unabated. When Celtic clinched the league title in memorable style with the 6-0 thumping of Kilmarnock in April, the manager described the team's display as encapsulating the whole campaign. Fittingly, Mulgrew was the stand-out performer that day. From left-back, he scored two and provided another two of the six goals. His dazzling display summed up his outstanding season.

He wasn't completely finished, however. In the final Glasgow derby of the season, Mulgrew opened Celtic's account in a comprehensive 3-0 victory with a thumping diving header. In forty-three games, he contributed eight goals, along with countless assists. It was a remarkable return from a defender, particularly someone who many had discounted as a mere squad player on his reappearance in Paradise. Now he was indispensible. His road to success speaks volumes about his resolve and willpower. It is a football fairytale and an excellent example to any player to maintain faith. Indeed, Neil Lennon sees parallels with his own football journey.

"Charlie is a great role model for a lot of younger players," he said. "The way his career has panned out, things didn't work out for him here early on, but he went down to England, forged a career for himself, and he never gave up. He's worked his way to the top of the game in Scotland, and he's a great example to the other young players. I had the same problem when I was a kid at Manchester City when I got released, and a lot of other top players have had the same situation and dealt with it, and gone on to have great careers. Charlie is enjoying his football and he deserves to be where he is just now.

"He has shown real leadership qualities and real consistency and quality in his play, whether it be set-piece delivery, defending, passing or his appreciation of the game – it's all there. He is near enough the complete footballer, where he can play in various positions and not look out of place. He has a good footballing brain as well, which is important. He's also a very good athlete and he works very hard on that side of the game."

Unlike his older colleague, James Forrest's career has followed a steady upward trajectory. Recruited into the Celtic Youth Academy when he was just ten-years-old, the Ayrshire Bhoy attended one of the club's development centres in Hamilton, where he was coached by Martin Miller, the current head of the Junior Academy.

As he progressed through the various age levels, the promising youngster was capped at youth level for Scotland, and that was where Neil Lennon first set eyes on him. When the Irishman took responsibility for Celtic's Development Squad during Tony Mowbray's time at the club, he got the opportunity to work with the player.

"I first saw him playing for Scotland Under-16s or Under-17s, on the telly against England," said the manager. "I remember James going up to the left-back, who had already played first-team football, and going right past him. I thought, 'That's impressive.' I thought he had something. I kept an eye on him, and then had him for a year when he was head and shoulders above anything, even in England."

Allied to an immense natural talent, Forrest also demonstrated a willingness to learn and a strong work ethic. When the Irishman took temporary charge of the first team in 2010, he was keen to give him the chance to shine on the big stage. At the start of May, he handed Forrest his first-team bow against Motherwell as a second-half sub-stitute. It was quite an introduction. He scored with almost his first touch, a delightful chip over the goalkeeper.

However, it was during Neil Lennon's first full season at the helm that James Forrest's blossoming talent was showcased. A series of exhilarat-ing performances in the opening weeks saw him become a firm fixture in the first-team squad, at the expense of more experienced players. If the plan was to stagger his entry into the top team, it was rendered impossible by his sparkling showings. By the campaign conclusion, despite several injuries, he had racked up twenty-five appearances, and earned his first Scotland cap against the Republic of Ireland.

Forrest's desire for excellence continued, and throughout season 2011/12 he was on fire, and no-one could douse the flames. He tormented defences with his touch, speed and skill, which was under-lined by a sensational showing in a 4-0 victory over Motherwell in September in which he bagged a brilliant brace. Yet, perhaps the most impressive facet of his performances was his ability to seize responsi-bility under challenging circumstances, normally a duty allocated to those with far greater experience.

As Celtic toiled at Rugby Park in October, the twenty-year-old took the game by the scruff of the neck, and was the inspiration behind a three-goal comeback which was to prove pivotal in the season. Neil Lennon described his display as "magnificent." It was performances such as this which prompted SFA technical director, Mark Wotte, to state that Forrest was the "light in the darkness" of Scottish football.

"I think he really matured," said the Hoops boss. "His level of performance in the games was of a very high standard, and he's a special talent. We love him here and the fans love him as he's an entertainer and an eliminator. He's a very exciting player, and it's a great result for our Academy and the work they have done with him in the previous years."

Celtic have been blessed with some wonderful wingers over the years – Jimmy Johnstone, Charlie Tully and, more recently, Aiden McGeady. They were entertainers, and firm favourites on the terraces. Neil Lennon believes James Forrest to be of a similar ilk.

"He's so explosive, he has great pace over fifteen or twenty yards, and now he can extend those runs over thirty to forty yards," he said. "This is part of the whole package with someone we think is going to be a very good player. The fans like wingers – I like wingers. He's a bit like your throwback winger, he likes to get to the byline at times or he can come inside to hurt teams. His football intelligence is improving, his touch is excellent and his passing's getting better. We hope he'll improve, and we aim to get him on the ball in very good areas. One-on-one, we want him to be direct, because he's hard to stop. It's wrong to compare him with the likes of Aiden McGeady but it's fair to say he's a bit more direct."

Younger players are usually prone to an element of rawness on the pitch, and this can take several seasons of competitive football to refine. However, Forrest has quickly matured. His awareness, decision-making and intelligence on the field belie his tender years.

"As well as good footballers, they are intelligent boys and they understand the game – and James Forrest is a classic example of that," said the Hoops boss. "He is twenty but his football appreciation is already very mature. I don't need to stand and talk to James for twenty minutes. He sees things in the game and makes right decisions, picks up good positions and knows where he is on the pitch, where to go with the ball and when he has to pass it, so he is a fine example of the intelligence we have in the squad."

Forrest's reputation has spread beyond the confines of Scottish football, with several Premier League clubs reportedly casting admiring glances in his direction. And in January 2012, he was identified by FIFA as one of the most exciting young players in football and a potential star of the year. Thirteen players in total were named on the list, including Thiago Alcantara of Barcelona, Gaston Ramirez of Bologna and Ahmed Musa, the Nigerian teenager who moved to CSKA Moscow for ten million Euros. Without wishing to saddle Forrest with extra hype, the manager believed he belonged in that sort of company.

"Every week I seemed to be talking about James but he's a wonderful player. I didn't want to build the kid up too much because that's not fair. We just wanted him to carry on with what he was doing. He's loving life here, he's enjoying his football and you can see that because he goes out on to the pitch and looks like a superstar in the making.

"He's such a level-headed boy. He just loves playing his football and with the type of player he is, he's a real asset for us and for Scotland. He really excites people. He's a throwback to the likes of Jimmy Johnstone. He's one we want to look after really well."

Late in the League Cup final, Forrest sustained severe bruising to a bone which ruled him out of the remainder of the season. Up to that point, he had been virtually an ever-present in the team, demonstrating that he had overcome a susceptibility to picking up hamstring niggles, a feature of his previous campaign. Although he missed out being on the pitch as the league title was confirmed, he had more than played his part in the success. The world is at his feet.

"James is just a precious talent and one we hope will be here for a long time," said the manager. "He's the type of player that gets you off your seat and we are very proud of the years he has been at Celtic and how he has come through our Academy. We are very pleased with his development so far, and we missed him a little bit over the last few weeks of the season. We have missed that dynamism and that rapier thrust he gives us from all positions, whether it's left wing, right wing or off the striker. He is a very intelligent young footballer with a huge future in front of him. James is an exceptionally good player and I think he could go and play anywhere."

EVERY successful team requires a strong leader on the pitch, someone who can shoulder responsibility, inspire and cajole. It's a vital function. Celtic's undisputed leader is Scott Brown. Although he didn't scoop any individual gongs in May 2012, the captain's contribution certainly didn't go unnoticed by Neil Lennon. Indeed, the manager is one of Brown's strongest supporters, always willing to underline his importance to the team. This viewpoint is shared by his team-mates, and that's no accident.

Much to his frustration, the midfielder missed around two months of the season as he had to undergo surgery for an ankle injury. However, he rapidly made up for lost time on his return as he helped propel the team to the title with a series of outstanding performances full of doggedness, determination and drive. This was Brown's fifth season at the club and, according to the Irishman, it was his most productive.

"Scott's not overlooked by us in terms of the backroom staff," he explained. "On and off the field he has been tremendous. I think he had his best season. Once he got through the surgery there was a spell between November and February where he was just on top form and he played very well in the remainder of the season as well. He's a very important player to the team, not just for what he brings off the field but he's a class player. He's a tremendous athlete and plays with great drive and leads the team very well.

"People talk about him being a good athlete but he reads the game very well and his football appreciation is good," said the manager. "I think he's a better footballer than people up here give him credit for and he certainly galvanised the team since he came back into the squad fit and healthy."

Despite having a reputation as a fierce competitor and having a combative style, Brown boasts an impressive disciplinary record, collecting just five yellow cards in all competitions in 2011/12. Susceptible to drawing the ire of referees as a youngster at Hibernian, it's another component of his game which he's improved.

"I think he conducts himself very well on the park," said the Hoops boss. "In terms of his discipline on the field, that has never been an issue for me. He was a little bit hot-headed earlier in his career but we all were. He's matured a lot quicker than most people have done, and I think he had to, with the responsibility of the armband. He's mentally and physically tough. In terms of personality, he's got more attributes than I had with his running power and his eye for a goal as well. I'm just very pleased with the way he's progressed in the role he's been given."

Although it's not his principal duty, Brown has received criticism for his lack of goals at Celtic. However, the midfielder chipped in with several crucial ones in 2011/12, particularly around January and February. At the same time, he emerged as being reliable in taking penalty-kicks, finally arresting Celtic's exasperating propensity to miss from twelve yards.

"There was a spell where he scored around three or four in a row and he took it upon himself to take the penalties. He was very consistent with that as well, and that shows the great leadership he has. He scored a great goal at St Mirren in January to cement a victory and it just shows that quality he has got, but his play in general has also been of a very high standard."

Celtic's squad has undergone wholesale changes during the manager's reign – but one constant has been Scott Brown's place in the team and his possession of the captain's armband. That's a measure of how highly he is rated behind the scenes.

"The extra responsibility of being captain means he's well respected in the dressing room by everyone. He's an excellent captain. I think he has the respect of the players in the dressing room, which obviously is very important at a big club."

Brown has gradually grown into the role of club skipper and having signed a new long-term deal in December 2011, he looks certain to be an integral part of the manager's future plans.

"He's taken on that responsibility himself," added the Hoops boss. "I think he knows how important it is to the club and I think he knows now what an important figure he is at the club. He's handled that ever so well."

Another player who repaid Neil Lennon's faith in his ability was Georgios Samaras. From zero to hero, the Greek almost mirrored Celtic's fortunes throughout the season. Derided in some quarters for persevering with the misfiring striker in the opening part of the campaign, the manager famously stated at the club's AGM in October that Samaras was the type of player who "could get me the sack." Despite that frank admission, the manager did not budge, for he knew Samaras had the talent. The question was how to extract it on a regular basis. Once that problem had been solved, Celtic had a formidable weapon in their arsenal. Cheers not jeers now greet his name in Paradise.

"My best decision of the season was possibly sticking with Georgios," said the manager. "He has shown magnificent character. At the start of the season, fans were turning on him very quickly but he believed in himself and we believed in him, and for four or five months of the season he was fantastic. I famously said that he was a gamble because he was so inconsistent but I made a decision to stick with him and give him a new contract. Then it was a matter of how to get the consistency out of him he had not shown in previous years.

"We had a long chat one night and he said he felt he had to play games and I said, 'That's fine as long as you play well' and that we would help him with that. There were times he did not want to play in the centre as he felt his best position was wide left and we had to find the balance of where we could fit him into the team. We did that and Georgios was fantastic for three or four months and nobody disputed his talent."

While Charlie Mulgrew and James Forrest took the individual plaudits, Celtic's title triumph was ultimately a vast collective effort, encompassing every member of the squad and the backroom staff. Although Neil Lennon chose his team from a core of players every week, over thirty players turned out for the top team. While their efforts may have been given scant coverage in comparison to higher-profile individuals, the manager is quick to recognise the importance of their input over the course of the campaign, particularly where injuries wreaked havoc at one stage. He is keen to acknowledge their contribution.

"All championship wins are a team effort," he said. "You do have your strong individuals who play most of the games and are the fulcrum of the team but it was a squad effort. Some players who came in when we needed them did brilliantly. Cha at times has played very well for us. Beram Kayal had his spell out of the team through injury, but when he played he was excellent. I have had my main nucleus of the team but the squad players who have come in have contributed immensely."

Neil Lennon never wavered from this mantra on collective effort even as he was crowned SPL Manager of the Year to add to his gong from the Scottish football writers. Clearly, it was a source of personal pride for the Irishman to be recognised for his coaching abilities, given all the adversity he had successfully overcome since taking the job, but he deflected all the praise directed at him on to his squad. He had put his faith in them – and they had delivered.

"I was delighted to pick up the Manager of the Year award as it is a privilege and an honour and sums up a season in which winning the SPL title meant everything to me. Individual honours are quite special but you cannot do it without the players. It makes me feel very proud but I'm proud of them, not myself. They are the players now. I have had my day. I'm the manager and it's my job to get the best out of them but what pleases me more is that they have repaid the faith and belief we have shown in them and now they believe in themselves.

"Individual awards are nice but any manager will tell you that you're only as good as your players, so me winning that award is just an indication of how well the players have played. The most important thing was winning the championship, for everyone concerned. There is good solidarity among the squad and good comradeship, which again you like to see among them. The atmosphere is good and the spirit is good. They stick together and they play for each other and play for the club, which is all we can ask for really."

Togetherness and team spirit is integral in any dressing room with designs on success. It creates a winning environment, where each player is willing to fight for one another to achieve the ultimate goal. Developing that united front was a pressing priority for the Hoops boss on his appointment to the hot seat. While the players he had inherited were talented enough footballers, they were not functioning well enough as a cohesive unit.

"When I took over we had Aiden McGeady, Artur Boruc, Robbie Keane and Diomansy Kamara. It was a really strong squad," he said. "But with this team there is more spirit and togetherness. They are a lot younger and hungrier. They are willing to give everything for the club and I love that about them. They never know when they are beaten. What I like most is their hunger and their motivation. The season has been fantastic. We work hard behind the scenes to make the preparation the best we can for the team. That has evolved over the two years and we learn from our mistakes."

Notably, this had been accomplished despite the diverse composition of the squad, with players hailing from all corners of the globe. This would normally be an impediment to constructing a harmonious and unified atmosphere – but not at Celtic. Here, team spirit is deep rooted. Several individuals had performed a major role in building this feeling of togetherness.

"There is a great spirit," said the manager. "We have some great characters in the dressing room in that respect in the likes of Scott, Charlie and Georgios. Every one of them has shown their personalities in one way or another. They are from different countries, different cultures, different religions and different ways of football, but they have all mixed and bought into the club, and I'm really pleased at the contribution of all of them."

Football
Focus

NEIL LENNON had waited over a month to get his hands on the SPL trophy – now his most pressing concern was not to drop it. Celtic had wrapped up the title in the emphatic 6-0 win over Kilmarnock at the start of April, but the trophy presentation had been delayed until the final home game of the season against Hearts in May, to allow a greater number of supporters to attend the celebrations. Having won the championship five times as a player, it was a piece of silverware which held special significance for the Irishman. However, raising it aloft as Celtic manager meant much more, and he was anxious not to ruin the moment by letting it slip from his grasp.

"I was thinking, 'Don't drop it!' It's quite an awkward one to lift because the handles are quite tight to the base of the trophy, so I just made sure I didn't drop it. But it was lovely. It's been a good friend to me over the years as a player so to finally get my hands on it as manager was brilliant."

It was the culmination of a perfect day in Paradise. Everything was in place for a party, and the players were determined to bring their best to the occasion and start the festivities with a victory. Although the title was in the bag, they wanted to produce a performance befitting of champions and end the season in style in front of a capacity Celtic Park crowd.

"I wanted them to finish the season in a fitting way," said the manager. "It was something we had waited a few years for, and everyone was looking forward to getting their hands on the trophy. But we had a game to play, and I wanted the team to finish the game in the style we had played all season."

That they did. It was a champagne showing. From the first whistle, Celtic were in fizzing form, with the fireworks provided by Gary Hooper. Scotland's top scorer was rampant and ruthless, bagging all five goals in a typically predatory performance as the Bhoys ripped apart the Tynecastle side 5-0, much to the delight of a jubilant home crowd.

"It was a tremendous individual performance from Gary and a great achievement," said the manager. "We played brilliantly on the day and won the game handsomely. It was a great way to finish the season. It was very pleasing. I asked the players to put on a performance for us and they did that, and I think the supporters enjoyed it. I wanted them to finish the season on a high and I wanted them to play entertaining football and win the game handsomely – and I got it all."

Celtic had transformed a fifteen-point deficit to a twenty-point lead by the end of the season. It was an extraordinary achievement. Not that it was necessary, but this was a final, resounding demonstration of why Celtic deserved to be crowned champions.

"We had been pretty much flawless in the league since October. We'd had a couple of defeats along the way, but the intensity and quality of the play for four or five months was excellent. We had broken the SPL clean-sheet record, we just fell one short of the goals we scored last year and we had the best disciplinary record. We won the league by twenty points, so it ticks all the boxes for me."

It had been a vast collective effort. The manager did not want anyone to miss out on the celebrations. Beram Kayal, a key figure in the first half of the season and, indeed, since the Irishman had taken the reins, had been absent since the turn of the year through an ankle injury and had fought ferociously to return before the end of the campaign. His persistence was rewarded when he entered the fray as a second-half substitute against Hearts, allowing him to end the season on the pitch.

"He was a little bit rusty obviously, but I wanted to give the players who had made big contributions the opportunity to play," said the manager. "Beram had been a huge player for us and, bar injury, he would have played a lot more for us this season. I was delighted with the performance, the professionalism and the quality of the players out there."

The championship was back where it belonged. There were joyful scenes as the players and backroom staff undertook a lap of honour around the stadium with the trophy they had long coveted. For some of the squad who had played their last game for the club, it was also a fond farewell, making it quite a moving moment.

Among those on the pitch was Neil Lennon, accompanied by his young son, Gallagher. As he received the adulation from fans, his achievements now started to sink in. This was a proud and poignant moment. Over the past two years he had endured and overcome the worst forms of adversity. This was a day to savour. He could not have wished for events to unfold in a better way. It was a fitting finale. For a short time, he could appreciate the success of the previous twelve months.

"Gallagher loves his football and I was happy to have him with me when the team received the SPL trophy, as happy as I know my own parents were to see me win that title as Celtic manager. It had been something I had been looking forward to very much, to be the manager of this club and take a team to the title is the best thing I had done in my professional career. The last few years had been difficult in terms of stuff I have had to deal with off the field, but the on-field stuff was brilliant. The players had done it, and in a style that I think the supporters appreciated and could relate to. So it was not just about me but about the players and the supporters – it was for them.

"It was very special. As a manager, it meant so much to me. It had been a tough season but to finish it off in that fashion was brilliant. Just the connection the players and supporters have now makes me very happy. I wanted it badly for the fans as they had been starved of success for two or three years, but to have it back in the trophy room was a great feeling. We could now reflect on what we had achieved. It was a fantastic feeling. I was delighted for the players and supporters, and I was delighted with the performance. It was a fitting way to end the season. The supporters were in good voice and it was a great day for the club."

Nevertheless, the Irishman isn't the type of character to stand still and seek satisfaction in past success. Amidst the celebrations, he was already pondering future challenges. Work for the 2012/13 season had already begun. The treble dream may have died with the defeats at Hampden to Kilmarnock and Hearts but, importantly, Celtic were in possession of the title. That had always been the main objective.

"It's been a bit of a rollercoaster but ultimately hugely rewarding," he added. "We deservedly won the title and obviously there is a tinge of disappointment with the cup competitions, where we felt at one stage we could have won the treble. It was a very hard thing to do but it shows how quickly the team had progressed. Instead of talking of challenging for the league we were talking about winning trebles now. So I am immensely satisfied. It augurs well for the future."

AS soon as Celtic clinched the title, Neil Lennon had one date fixated in his mind – July 31. That's the first date of the UEFA Champions League third qualifying round. Wary of inviting unnecessary pressure, there is an understandable reluctance to publicly air all his objectives for the forthcoming campaign, but he is happy to divulge his two aims of progress in Europe along with a successful title defence.

Returning the Hoops to Europe's premier club competition is a major aspiration of the Irishman. Four years have elapsed since Celtic last reached the group stages of the tournament. That's too long in the manager's opinion. Notwithstanding the obvious financial benefits, he believes a club of Celtic's stature belongs among that company and like any coach with ambition, he wants to test himself at the top level.

"When you have ambitions and you make them public to the press, people try to ridicule them or knock them down," he explained. "Obviously we have targets and that is to defend the championship and we have the Champions League qualifiers, which is where we really want to be as a club, where I want to take the players and where I would like to be as a coach. That's the next step. We want to play at the big table. You start a plan for next year. The Champions League qualifiers are at the forefront of my mind, and obviously trying to get players in as quickly as I can.

"We have two qualifiers and the first one is our main focus. Can we hit the ground running, as these games come so early and we have to be at our best. It's really important we get the pre-season and close-season right for that. One of our first competitive games will be a Champions League qualifier so we have a lot of hard work in front of us to get ready for that."

Indeed, work on conditioning the squad in readiness for the game started during the normal season. The realisation Celtic could face a team with a substantial fitness advantage at that early juncture in the campaign was motive behind this strategy.

"It is a very difficult scenario when your first competitive game is going to be a Champions League qualifier," said the Hoops boss. "You could get a team who may be five or six games into their season, and who are up to match-speed. It is always a tightrope which you are walking, so we worked with the players over the last few weeks of the season, with routines for them to do over the summer. Obviously we want them to have a break as well, they have earned that, but we want them to come back in at a pretty decent level of fitness for the start of pre-season again."

Match sharpness will not be the sole concern, however. In addition to preparing players physically for the fixture, the manager is aiming to have recruited several new faces to the squad by that point. Again, it will be a hectic summer for the manager on this front.

Despite creating a championship-winning side, it will be a summer of change within the Celtic squad. Reducing the size of the playing pool whilst increasing quality will form the foundation of the strategy. A number of players whose contracts were set to expire were allowed to leave, and they were joined by several others. In their place, the Hoops boss hoped to attract individuals who could enhance the existing group.

"I was looking to trim the squad. It was a bit clogged up so I was hoping to trim a few players and add a bit of quality here and there. We were pretty happy with the nucleus of the squad. We had a few meetings along the way and tried to single out a few players who could come in and make us better."

From Fraser Forster in the last line of defence to Gary Hooper at the spearhead of the attack, Celtic's squad possesses a youthful vitality. Since Neil Lennon took the job, he has tended to sign players in the younger age-group bracket. Was that design or accident?

"It's a bit of both really," he explained. "The club want to find these players and try and improve them and have a resalable value because that's the way we have to work. At the time, I wanted to get some more experienced players in but; one, they didn't want to come and, two, they wanted too much money. And I enjoy working with the players. They are no problem to work with. None of them are confrontational in that aspect. They come in and enjoy what they do, and it's great watching them develop into top players. You get a lot of satisfaction from that."

Adding experience to a predominantly youthful dressing room would be preferential but not essential.

"You have to go in with an open mind," explained the Irishman. "Ideally, we would like a couple more experienced players but it's never set in stone. You go with the best option you can get at the time for the best deal, so we are working hard again on bringing a bit of quality into the club, whether they are young, old or experienced. If we feel they will be an asset to the club, we will do the deal."

Some had speculated that Rangers' (or the club that succeeds them following liquidation) current financial woes might result in a reduction in investment in new players. That's something the manager completely refutes.

"The club has its own strategy," he insisted. "I had a meeting with Peter Lawwell and he showed how we are moving the club forward in that respect so regardless of how strong or how weak Rangers are, that won't change our mindset."

Informing players that their time at Celtic is at an end is a difficult process, particularly for those who have served the club with distinction over many years.

"That is difficult," admitted the manager. "You have people like Mark Wilson, who has been a great servant to the club. Other players knew in their own minds that their time was up so that makes it a little bit easier and they understand the situation, but it's never easy as the majority of the players have made important contributions to the team and the club during their time here."

Wilson, who was the longest-serving player at the club, left after his contract wasn't renewed. Following a magnificent campaign in the manager's first season at the helm, which included a winning goal in a Glasgow derby, a persistent knee problem hindered his progress over the next twelve months. In recognition of his efforts over the previous six-and-a-half years, the lifelong Celtic supporter was given the chance to captain the team in one last appearance in Paradise during the 1-0 over St Johnstone in May.

"Mark thoroughly deserved it and I think the fans wanted to show their appreciation to him as well," said the manager. "We brought him off with about fifteen minutes to go and he got a standing ovation – and rightly so. He's tremendous. I don't know how many titles he's won, maybe three or four. He had a fantastic season last year in my first season – I think he scored four goals from right-back – but his performances were exceptional. We decided to offer him a new contract then and keep him on as we felt he deserved it, but he has been curtailed with injuries since. He had surgery around Christmas time and that really held him back in terms of this season. But he can look back on his Celtic career with an enormous amount of pride. He was a very consistent performer who gave everything for the club."

Just as important as player recruitment, though, is preventing the plunder of Celtic's prized assets. Several teams in the English Premier League have reportedly shown an interest in the likes of Gary Hooper and James Forrest. With a ready supply of cash in England's top flight, a big-money offer may transpire in the future. Having worked hard to assemble a title-winning team, this is a scenario the manager is naturally keen to avoid. He believes the experience of winning as a Celtic player, and the subsequent adulation from a passionate fanbase, will be a strong carrot for remaining in Paradise.

"I think the realisation in winning the championship and the feeling they get from days like that and from clinching the title at Kilmarnock, you would be hard-pressed to find that feeling and connection with supporters anywhere else, certainly in Britain," said the Hoops boss. "We have created new heroes here over the past two years and they have become very popular with the fans. I don't think they would get that mutual feeling with many other clubs. I think they enjoy the environment they are playing in and the style of football we try to play, and I'm very proud of them."

One of the main motives behind the current transfer strategy is to allow space for the club's home-grown talent to flourish. Historically, many of the greatest to wear the Hoops came from within – the Kelly Kids, the Quality Street Gang – and there was a special affinity between them and the supporters. Bringing through another Jimmy Johnstone, Paul McStay or Aiden McGeady has always been an aspiration but it is a route Celtic are increasingly looking to follow. Quite simply, because of the disparity in TV deals, Celtic, for the moment, find it tough to compete financially with the big-spending clubs of the English Premier League and other top-flight leagues on the continent. This has led to greater investment in the club's Youth Academy, with Forrest the most recent example of this approach bearing fruit. His rapid progress has been inspiring, and there are several other young players waiting in the wings.

"That's the aim," said the manager. "It's a really important facet of the club. We want to cultivate our own players and these guys coming through have a real affinity for the club, a love for it. I think it's important that the fans see this as well – that the club are producing good, young players. We have got two or three who are bubbling under nicely who will hopefully have more of an impact on the first-team squad next season. We have a good crop of young players coming through who we have to drip-feed in slowly."

There seems to be grounds for optimism, judging by the exploits of several youngsters in the past twelve months. No-one will forget Dylan McGeouch's dream home debut for the club. Six minutes after coming on as substitute, the midfielder embarked on a solo run from his own half, jinked past a number of challenges and drilled the ball home. It was Celtic's goal of the season. At the end of April, supporters got their first glimpse of Tony Watt as he made his top-team bow as a second-half replacement at Fir Park. With the game goal-less, the young striker bagged a brilliant brace to help Celtic record a 3-0 victory. In the game that wrapped up the championship against Kilmarnock, young Czech midfielder, Filip Twardzik, impressed after coming on for Scott Brown, cleverly assisting Joe Ledley for a goal with a sublime flick.

"We have had Dylan who has made good contributions, and who scored a great goal against St Mirren, probably one of the goals of the season," said the Irishman. "We have already seen the emergence of Tony Watt, who was a real bonus for us. He was up training with us for the last three or four weeks and we were hoping to give him game time before the end of the season and he was excellent. Filip Twardzik was a real nice surprise at Kilmarnock. I thought he was excellent in the second half and we know what a good player he can be. Filip would have played more but he got injured in the Youth Cup final, so these three will be knocking on the door for a first-team place next year.

"Then you've got the 19s who were very successful – the like of Callum McGregor, Jackson Irvine and Marcus Fraser. Unfortunately, Paul George got a really bad injury so he will be out for a wee bit but we have high hopes for him, too."

Making the breakthrough is one thing, but repeating Forrest's feats and becoming a regular pick is a far more formidable test. It is the greatest hurdle to overcome. That is the next challenge which awaits Celtic's young guns.

"You might not see them initially but we are hoping to develop these players on into being regular Celtic players," the Hoops boss said. "They have had a fantastic time of it over the two or three years at Under-19 level but the real hard work starts for them now. It's what I want – one or two more coming through. It's hard getting there but the hardest part is staying there. We don't want them just to be here for a cameo role here and there, we want them to be in the squad consistently now for the next two or three years. The hardest thing is staying there on a consistent level and that's the challenge that awaits these boys now."

Young players guided by a young manager, but one who has learned much in the past two years. Neil Lennon was only thirty-nine when he took charge of Celtic on a permanent basis. It was his first managerial post, and there were doubts if he had the experience for such a pressurised position. Not now. Confirmation comes in the form of the green and white ribbons adorning the championship silver. Nonetheless, with practice comes knowledge, and the Irishman has naturally evolved as a coach in the past two years. Nothing can prepare for the onset of adversity. He faced it at Rugby Park as Celtic toiled 3-0 down – and survived.

"You never stop learning," he said. "I understood why the club, the board in particular, wanted a more experienced man in beside me. I was a rookie in a hugely challenging environment and job but I've learned a lot. When you're fifteen points behind in a two-horse race, your back is against the wall. It's the lowest you can get. I've proved to myself I can handle these situations. I now have the championship to my name and that means a huge amount to me. Maybe if I hadn't won it, I wouldn't be in a job now — such is the environment that we work in because the standards are set so high. That's given me a lot of confidence going into next year.

"I have learned a lot but I'm sure every other manager, regardless of what age they are or how experienced they are, will make mistakes as they go along, or they will be perceived by other people as having made mistakes. But that's just the nature of the job, I don't take much notice of that as the people who matter to me are obviously the people I work for and the supporters. I'm sure they will be first to let me know."

AFTER hoisting the trophy high into the air in Celtic Park, Neil Lennon strode purposefully over to the corner of the stadium occupied by the Green Brigade and placed it on the pitch in front of them. With this gesture, he was recognising their role in the title triumph. Both at home and away, this colourful group of fans had steadfastly supported the team over the course of the previous two years. In Paradise, they had helped instigate a more vibrant, carnival atmosphere, particularly through their singing of songs like, *Just Can't Get Enough* and doing The Huddle, which have now become as much a part of the Celtic repertoire as *The Celtic Song* and *You'll Never Walk Alone*.

This was important to the manager. He noticed these things, and he wanted to show his appreciation.

"It was just a thank you to the Green Brigade really, certainly that section, who have supported the team through thick and thin," he said. "Whether they do it through humour, song or just the energy they bring to the stadium, they have changed the culture. It's a fun place to come to for supporters and the atmosphere over the last two years in some of the big games has been fantastic. They have been the catalyst for that.

"They do it with a bit of humour and colour and they have brought that to Celtic Park. 'The Huddle' has been a phenomenon at times and *Just Can't Get Enough* has been the symbol song. It has really resonated throughout the stadium at times and has really caught fire. Everywhere you went, you would hear it. Even though some of the games are a little bit flat at times, these guys just sing away and do their best to get the rest of the stadium going. They sing non-stop, they add colour. Sometimes they are a little bit controversial but in the main they have behaved themselves impeccably. So for me it was just a thank you to them for all of their support over two years."

On the day of his appointment, the manager asserted his intention to "bring the thunder back" to Paradise. By assembling an attacking, entertaining and, ultimately, winning team, he hoped to create a Celtic side which supporters could identify with and take pride in. He wanted to create a sense of unity around the club again, and there's no greater visible demonstration of unity than 60,000 fans partaking in a mass Huddle. He has delivered.

"What pleases me as much as anything is the connection that the supporters have with the players," he said. "They have the songs for individual players, and we have built new heroes here at the club and the supporters can identify with that. When we go away from home it's almost like a carnival atmosphere. The noise, the singing, the pride – it's all there now. I'm delighted with that. It was missing for a few years, and I think more than anything, the fans have their pride back.

"I love seeing the Huddle. It's an amazing spectacle. I just love it when they are all joining in and are all happy and singing. It gives you a sense of satisfaction, there is no doubt about it."

Neil Lennon holds a special bond with the Celtic support, stemming from his days as a pivotal player and captain in one of the greatest Celtic teams of the modern era. At a basic level, he is a supporter of the club himself and he can empathise with their emotions. It is certainly an advantage for a Celtic manager.

"It's important that I have a connection with the supporters, for the sake of the team more than anything else – for them to identify with someone," he explained. "I'm lucky with my background and my playing career that I have a deep association with the club. Sometimes that can work against you but even during the tough period, when we were way behind in the league, the majority of the fans were right behind us and I can't thank them enough for that."

This is another reason why he wanted to highlight their contribution. The Hoops boss believes their backing, particularly in times of adversity, helped determine the destiny of events on the pitch.

"Even that day when we were 3-0 down at Kilmarnock, the fans were singing, encouraging and pushing the team on. We got something out of the game that day and they played a huge part – and have done since. Certainly at the game against Rangers at the end of December, they were brilliant. The Hearts game when Fraser saved the penalty, they were tremendous that day as well.

"That game was really tight and a lot of times the games have been like that. What I've sensed has left the stadium a little bit is that nervousness and anxiety. It was less apparent this year more than any other year really, when the team might have been struggling to get a goal. The crowd stay with them for the majority of the time until we manage to make the breakthrough. Normally there was an anxiety creeping in from the stand down on to the pitch. That was less and less noticeable this year and was very important."

While the manager was fully aware of the passion and zeal of the Celtic support, he believes the players are now conscious of this fact. Indeed, how could they fail to be, after witnessing the joy and pride etched across the fans' faces as Celtic reclaimed the championship.

"The day at Kilmarnock when we won the league, it really hit home to the players how much it means to so many people and how much it means to them personally," said the Irishman. "It was the epitome of the two years that we have been here, the way the team played and the backing the support gave us from start to finish. The joy around the stadium that day will live long in the memory, not just for me but the players as well."

The Celtic fans' enthusiasm is in evidence outside as well as inside the ground, no more so than during the recent visit of children from the Good Child Foundation – popularly known as the Thai Tims. Supporters had taken the youngsters from rural Thailand to their hearts after watching them perform Celtic songs on the Internet, taught to them by Celtic fan, Paul Lennon, and his wife, Pun. As their fame grew, the manager and players also became aware of this remarkable phenomenon. It was not long before the campaign got underway to bring them to Paradise. During their stay in April, they performed twice to fans in Celtic Park and to a sold-out Glasgow Royal Concert Hall, as well as visiting Belfast. Meeting the children a few days after beating Rangers in the final derby of the season was another highlight for Neil Lennon.

"It was lovely," he said. "The connection with the Thai Tims is absolutely wonderful and we were all looking forward to their visit. The kids were great and are such a phenomenon now at the club. I was really looking forward to meeting them and off the back of a great weekend it was a lovely way to start the week

"They have really captured the hearts of the people and caught the imagination. We all enjoy the songs. We all enjoy the joy that the kids have singing the songs and we all enjoy the joy they bring to the supporters and ourselves. They had enhanced the club no end. I think they brought a lot of joy and happiness to a lot of supporters not just here in Scotland but around the world."

Events like this remind Neil Lennon why Hoops supporters are quite extraordinary. They are the reason Celtic are 'more than a club.' He was thrilled at delivering them some silverware.

"Our fans are pretty special," said the manager. "They have been starved of success and thankfully the players have managed to bring that success back to them, and everyone is looking forward to the future now. The club is on a good footing, but without the supporters we would just be a normal, run-of-the-mill club."

One year earlier, the manager had addressed fans inside Celtic Park after losing the league on the final day of the season, promising them it was "just the beginning." He was now a championship-winning manager. But the story remains incomplete.

"We would like more of the same." the Irishman said. "We are going to defend our title as best we can and hopefully make inroads into the Champions League. That will be very important to our season, but it's very early when the games come and they are very difficult. However, we will do all we can to try and bring European football here as well."

Over the past twelve months, Neil Lennon had experienced adversity on and off the pitch, cup disappointments and sorrow at the death of a close friend. But it had ended with a silver lining.

A Season In Quotes

Chapter 1: Starting Over

"There was a great support out in Australia. It just shows the size of this club, with the following we get around the world. It was great for them and also great for us. So it worked out well. For the likes of the new lads, Kelvin Wilson and Adam Matthews, they maybe never realised how big the club was so it was maybe a bit of an eye-opener for them. I think the boys who were here last season already knew how big a club this is from seeing the fans before."

CHARLIE MULGREW

"I've enjoyed it since the day I walked in the door. The boys made me feel really welcome, the training was very good and the management had been brilliant. Everyone knows that Celtic are a massive club but you don't realise how big it is until you actually move here. The biggest thing is the support really. The fans love you if you play for

Celtic, so that's been a big help to me really. The fans are really special. They are great supporters and that's the biggest thing I noticed. We went to Australia in pre-season and packed every stadium, so that just shows how big the fan base is. I knew it was big but it's surpassed my expectations. I thought it was crazy. There were people waiting for you in the airports on the other side of the world. Every footballer wants to play in front of passionate fans and there are no better fans than Celtic supporters so I was very excited about the season ahead."

ADAM MATTHEWS

"The jet-lag and different time-zones were hard work at first. At Derby County, we'd do three or four hours on a coach maybe but that was it. To go from that to twenty-four hours on a plane was completely different but I enjoyed it. Training in different climates and conditions is something you normally get used to quickly, but this was a bigger journey so jet-lag was a bit of a problem. But the medical staff and the coaches were aware of that and were going through the same transition sleeping wise. It was a good test for us, though. It was great experience and a valuable exercise to play the teams we did. Travelling to the other side of the world and playing in front of fans who don't normally get to see us play was definitely the highlight for me. We went to a few functions while we were there and got the chance to meet the fans before and after training sessions. They're just as passionate and dedicated as the people over here so to get the fantastic response that we did was unforgettable. Hopefully we left them with some sort of impact so they want to keep getting up early to watch our matches."

KRIS COMMONS

"Me and Woodsy [Stevie Woods, goalkeeping coach] had spoken almost every day over the summer so I think there was a great sense of relief in the end when it finally got sorted. It had been dragging on for a while, especially with Celtic's pre-season, and then we went to America after that so numerous things kept setting us back. Some days it was just general chat because we get on really well, but at times it was aiming towards getting me back up to Celtic. We worked hard over the summer to make this happen and I couldn't have been happier."

FRASER FORSTER

Chapter 2: Slowing Down

"When I saw Emilio fall I knew it wasn't great. It was more in the way he fell rather than the actual challenge – it was very, very harsh. It was nobody's fault, it was just the way he went down and put all the pressure on one side of his body. It's not nice to see it happen to anyone, never mind one of your own team-mates. Then you get the replays on the TV as well showing it over and over. It was especially unfortunate for Emilio because he had been playing really well. He had fitted in well and won all those Player of the Year awards the previous season. He looked as though he was about to kick-start this one the way he ended the last, so it was a blow to him and the team."

SCOTT BROWN

"Emilio was a very important player for us and did very well in 2010/11. It had been a big loss to us not having him in the team because he has a very big affect on us all. He was unlucky in the Aberdeen game but that didn't give us an excuse for losing games after that. We had to adapt and change our rhythm to be able to deal with that. When we lost a game the problem belonged to everyone, not just the defenders or the strikers. We had to work as a team because football is a team sport and we had 11 players."

KI SUNG YUENG

"The pressure was even more because we had a bad start, but the players wanted to play for the manager, we were behind him. There was no split in the dressing room. We wanted to play and get results for him. I didn't know where the rumours had come from, but it wasn't the manager's fault. As players, we needed to look at ourselves. We had let him down. One half we played well, the other we were a shadow of the team. So it wasn't just the gaffer, we had to look within ourselves."

ADAM MATTHEWS

"In some of the defeats we had played good football. Against St Johnstone we had chances to kill the game. We had been unlucky in some of them. We hadn't been that clinical. We had had a couple of chances and hadn't been putting them away, but as long as we were creating we should have got the wins. It was frustrating. We looked at videos of games and saw ourselves playing good stuff but not killing teams off. It's hard to coach things like that. We were playing well but the points were not there. From then until the end of the season, getting the points was more important than playing good football. You can blame strikers or the defence. You can point the finger at a lot of things. But it was basically doing more as a team and not forgetting you're a unit. We needed to work harder for each other."

JOE LEDLEY

"The injuries at the start of the season might have had a part to play in some of our results, but it's hard to put your finger on it. People say a set back-four is important but we train with each other every day and we know each other's game. We play a lot alongside each other and we all bring different things to the squad. It might have something to do with it but I don't think you just blame it on that. But it was great having the guys back to strengthen the squad again, it helped us all."

CHARLIE MULGREW

Chapter 3: Turning Point

"The turning point was Rugby Park. Everyone knows the Kilmarnock game was massive for us. We came from 3-0 down to draw 3-3 against all the odds, and then to go on from there and to go undefeated for twenty-six games in a row was brilliant."

SCOTT BROWN

"The gaffer was right to have a go at us. We didn't turn up. We couldn't score. We couldn't defend. I came off injured at half-time and the gaffer had just said to the players to go out and prove everyone wrong."

GARY HOOPER

"At half-time it was the worst I have ever felt in a game of football. Things just didn't go our way and Kilmarnock managed to get three goals from the three chances they had. It was a good feeling when the goal went in but it was relief more than anything. We wanted a winner and we were really disappointed not to get it, especially because I got the goal quite early on. There were still about ten minutes left, but in the end it was good to come back and get a point against the odds."

CHARLIE MULGREW

"Everyone was disappointed in the changing room when we were 3-0 down. We shouldn't be losing like that against any team. But we came out and the fans were still behind us, even though we were 3-0 down and ten points behind. That was the turning point. If we had lost it might have been different, but we came back and got a draw and that was vital. We always had belief and knew that we had players to come back from injury. We also knew Rangers would drop points and we'd need to capitalise on that. We did that and showed good character."

JAMES FORREST

"It was a massive turning point in our season. Being 3-0 down at half-time, the changing room wasn't the best place to be, but as we came out the fans gave us a massive lift and that showed in our second-half performance. They make a massive difference. There is nothing better, not just when you're winning but when you're losing and when you hear the fans cheering and supporting the team. It gives you a massive boost and you can tell that it means as much to them as it does to you."

ADAM MATTHEWS

"That was a big game for us and a really big turning point in the season. I've talked about it a few times with the family and they have always said that was the game where you could see we had changed. It sounds weird, but I think we needed that result to go the way it did. If we had beaten Kilmarnock by three or four goals, I'm not sure the penny would have dropped. It really helped galvanise the boys and drove us on. It brought us together and really helped us believe we could win the league. It was massive."

ANTHONY STOKES

Chapter 4: Fifteen To Won

"We were fifteen points behind going into Motherwell. It's a hard place to go and they're a tough team. It was 1-1 when I got on. Stokesy put a great ball across and I couldn't miss. I if I did, everyone would have went crazy at me!"

GARY HOOPER

"The Motherwell game was a must-win for us. That was when our run began so that was another turning point of the season. We were 1-0 down at one point, I wasn't playing, I was watching on TV. We got the two goals though, and Hoops scored near the end so that was massive for us. We kicked on and went on that good run. We were fifteen points behind at the start of November and we were devastated with the gap. We knew we had a lot of games to go, though, and we still had to play Rangers a few times, so we knew it wasn't over. We wanted to knuckle down and we believed in ourselves. We knew we should have been doing better because we have good players. In the end we proved that."

JOE LEDLEY

"We managed to turn it around by winning games and getting the points when we would have been dropping them earlier in the season. We were going away from home and winning really hard games and that showed the strength and character in the team. We had been winning games in the last minute and getting points when things weren't going our way and that's really important over the course of a season."

CHARLIE MULGREW

"Most of the lads will look at the derby games as turning points. I was injured for a while but looking on as an outsider, the Kilmarnock game when we were 3-0 down and came back, and the Hearts game when Fraser saved the penalty, are the two that stick in my mind. Those were moments when we needed big performances and players to stand up and be counted. Those two games were massive turning points and showed what we're all about. There were a few performances early on in the season when we weren't quite at it, and when you play for Celtic and don't win games, you are almost guaranteed Rangers will win every week, so we fell behind. But as far as morale and team spirit, there was always a belief that if we could put a run together we'd be there or thereabouts."

KRIS COMMONS

"We always knew we had the players. We never panicked. It was very important that we didn't change much despite the poor run of results, and stuck to things which we believe we felt was the right path for success. It was only the key to tell the players to work a bit harder for each other. Sometimes, it's easy to blame the defence for conceding goals but we started defending from the front as well. And once we started doing that we started to play so much better. I felt we could go on a run. It was just a matter of gaining confidence and getting more top players on form."

JOHAN MJALLBY

"It was a great achievement, twenty games and twenty wins – that's unbelievable, whatever league you are playing. It's nice, especially if you look back and we were fifteen points behind at one point. We turned it around and it was a great achievement from the lads. All the boys were buzzing. Even the lads who weren't playing, as there is a good team spirit here and everyone was in it together. Obviously we've had ups and downs but every club has that and we got our dip out of the way early doors, we kicked on and have not looked back, so that had been a good thing."

KELVIN WILSON

"I couldn't pick out one game that turned things around for us but if you look back to the game we drew 0-0 with Hibs, we were all very low after that. But only a few days later we played in Europe and beat Rennes at home. Then we went away to Motherwell and that was a massive game for us because they were challenging our position in the table. We beat them, and that gave us confidence. And a few weeks later we beat St Mirren 5-0 at home – that was a really good afternoon. We had just started a run at that time and that pushed us on and helped us a lot. There were a few big results for us around that time, and even though I didn't play against Kilmarnock, coming back from 3-0 to get a point helped the guys who played, their confidence grew."

GEORGIOS SAMARAS

"We knew we were going through a rocky patch and were worried about getting our form back. We just tried to work on the football as we knew what we were capable of. We knew what the gap was and were confident we could do it by the end of the season. I was just amazed we managed to turn it around in four or five weeks."

ANTHONY STOKES

Chapter 5: Euro Zone

"This season has been enjoyable and the European games stand out for me. That's where you want to be – playing against the best. That was the big plus for me. We did really well in the game in Udinese and that's the type of match that gives us a lot of hope for the future. We only got a draw but we could have won it as we had a few chances, but it was a good experience for us. We improved as we went along in the Europa League and were unlucky not to reach the last thirty-two. The Europa League was good for the lads as a lot of us hadn't played in it before and it's given us the experience. Hopefully we can take that on in the Champions League."

JAMES FORREST

"Europe was massive for us. We didn't have a brilliant run, but it really helped our confidence. We played against some very good sides and got some great results for such a young team. We were on a bad run at the time, so we needed something like that to dig us out of a hole and get us going again."

ANTHONY STOKES

"We proved in a tough group that we can compete in Europe. Apart from one or two decisions that didn't go our way, we could maybe have qualified for the last thirty-two of the Europa League. Each year you want to do better, and a run in the Champions League would be great. It is important to do everything we can to prepare for the qualifiers and get in among that again. That would be massive for everyone here."

CHARLIE MULGREW

Chapter 6: Neighbourhood Watch

"It was a disappointing day, getting sent off and losing 4-2. We never got going. We never played well and the first goal is always important. Rangers managed to get that. We did come back and go 2-1 up, but in the second half we never turned up. It was very disappointing."

CHARLIE MULGREW

"It was a brilliant way to end the year and it was a great team performance. It's always nice to beat your rivals, and especially to score the winning goal. I thought we deserved to win. When the goal went in, it lifted everyone and the whole team. It was a brilliant night and the fans were fantastic. You expect that in the derbies, though, because the Celtic supporters are the best fans. They have been brilliant with me ever since I signed for the club and they were brilliant on Twitter after the game, sending me their wishes and congratulating me. I really appreciated it."

JOE LEDLEY

"We had been fifteen points behind but that result against Rangers made it nine wins on the trot and showed how much we turned things around. We were happy with our form in November and December."

ADAM MATTHEWS

"We were a bit disappointed not to win at Ibrox. The lads were a bit down. But we were down to nine men and we managed a great come-back to make it to 3-2 but it wasn't to be that day."

SCOTT BROWN

"It was great for the team but personally I was delighted to get my goal. It was the first of the season and it was certainly long overdue after what was a long, hard season. To win the way we did, keep a clean sheet and score three magnificent goals was the icing on the cake for a very good season for the club. We had gone into the game with the mindset it was a cup final because they had already beaten us twice in the season. For us it was a must-win game. Everything gearing towards that game was about winning, and winning emphatically, and we managed it in the end."

KRIS COMMONS

Chapter 7: Campaign Supernova

"We went down to Kilmarnock and we were all in good spirits. Sitting on the bus we were all looking forward to the game. We had quite a fit team as well. Charlie started it off and he was unbelievable from the first minute to the last. To win 6-0 on the day was just incredible."

SCOTT BROWN

"The 6-0 win over Kilmarnock was an incredible occasion. The first half was just sensational – the fans, the singing, the atmosphere. And the way we played, the tempo we played at, to come in at 4-0 was just a remarkable shift from the lads. There are only a few occasions when I have forgotten about the game for a few milliseconds and just had a look around. There was one song when all the stands were singing to one another and the hairs on the back of my neck just stood up.

I got goosebumps, it was just incredible. The only other time that's happened was when we played Rangers at home in 2010/11 when the stadium did the Huddle when the score was at 3-0. That was amazing and was great to be part of."

KRIS COMMONS

"You work hard all season and to become champions in the style we did as well was something special. It was absolutely brilliant. The fans were terrific. To sell out three-quarters of the stadium away from home would never really have happened anywhere else. It was a great day and it couldn't have gone any better than it did on the pitch. It was an unbelievable atmosphere for the full ninety minutes, all the fans were singing. There was a real party atmosphere so it was just good that the lads could repay the fans and give them a performance like that. Obviously it was good after the game. I had won the league at Norwich but it's hard to compare the two really. There was a brilliant atmosphere after the game. You just work hard for so much of the season, so to win the league so comfortably in the end is absolutely brilliant."

FRASER FORSTER

"This is why you play football – to win things and the ultimate prize is to win the league. We were delighted to have done it this year and we did it in some style. You could see from the deliveries, the defenders were willing to go for it and it was a real team performance. That sums up the club at that time – we are a real team who worked hard for each other and it was all about winning the league at Kilmarnock. The fans were great but they're not just like that when we win things, when times are bad they are also still there and that shows they are real supporters through thick and thin. They deserved a party."

GLENN LOOVENS

"It had been a long time coming. We knew we would win the league finally but it was great to finish it in style. We were tremendous and the players had been brilliant. They had turned it around and showed how they are mentally strong. Some outside the club had questioned that but now the team are there, it's well-deserved and hopefully we can keep them together for a long time. They showed their true talent at Kilmarnock and how well they could play. Over the season they had been tremendous. They were so mentally strong and had worked so hard for one another to come back from when we were fifteen points behind. When we first came in, especially Neil, we knew we had to turn things around as we hadn't won the league for years. And now we had won the championship and that had always been the main focus. You could see from the scenes how much it meant to everybody."

JOHAN MJALLBY

Chapter 8: Hampden Heartache

"The League Cup final was a very big game and a chance for me to win something. It was very important to me before the game and I was very disappointed at full-time when we lost. Every player wants to win trophies and I was very excited about the thought of possibly doing that. But we didn't turn up and if you do that in cup finals you will not win anything. At the end of the day we could have won but we didn't take our chances, and that's why we lost. We know we didn't do well enough and we were all annoyed at ourselves. We were the better side and we didn't win when we should have. We had a lot of chances, though, and we could have done better, but we were unlucky so we had to move on. I don't think we had any pressure on us before the game but Kilmarnock also did well. We had to give them credit, they did their best and they got the winning goal."

VICTOR WANYAMA

"Everyone was devastated. We couldn't believe how we lost it, we let ourselves down and we let the fans down. The gaffer knew we were disappointed, and he was disappointed himself, but we all knew we could do better. We knew we were capable of putting those chances away on a different day. It was just very frustrating it didn't come off on such a big occasion. We were devastated that we lost the same cup again. We had a big chance to win it and we dominated the game – especially in the second half as we had lots of chances to open the scoring, but it wasn't to be. We couldn't put them away and we suffered for it. I don't think it was complacency or too much pressure, I just think we were unlucky. The chances we had, and the penalty shout at the end, those would come off for us on other days, but not this one. We could have done with that bit of luck to come out on top."

JOE LEDLEY

"The Kilmarnock keeper made some great saves. I thought we domi-nated the game and played well, but we just couldn't put the ball in the back of the net. We had chances from early on. Hoops had one and nine times out of ten he would put it away. But we kept on creating plenty of chances. Even in the second half, I thought we had sustained pressure before they went up the park and scored. You just had to congratulate Kilmarnock. At the end of the day, they were the winners and well done to them."

ANTHONY STOKES

"All the players were disappointed as we wanted the double and we were good enough to do it but we couldn't win, so I think everyone should be disappointed. It's a big disappointment, and I couldn't understand the referee's decision, but we should have scored more goals, especially my chances. I think we played well but Hearts always did the usual thing of having nine men behind the ball and it's very hard to break this down. We played well enough but they made two chances and scored while we didn't and that was the difference."

KI SUNG YUENG

Chapter 9: Keeping The Faith

"No one in Scottish footballing history has had to contend with this level of pressure while trying to do their job. Neil has shown tremendous strength of character and resilience and we will continue to support him in any way we can."

PETER LAWWELL

"He's still a young manager and is still learning the game itself, but he's been great for all of us and he's brought out the best in a lot of the young players here. He has been vital."

CHARLIE MULGREW

"This title was more for the gaffer than anyone else. What he's been through this season and last, it's not very nice for anyone, but he's dealt with it really well and taken it on his chin. He's got stronger and stronger and went out in every game to prove everybody wrong. His all-round game planning and coaching, along with the coaches he has brought in, have all been brilliant. We all look forward to training and we come in to try and thrive to be better, and pretty much everything has improved in the last two years."

SCOTT BROWN

"The manager has been great for us and he has been working hard through difficult times. It hasn't been easy for him and I know he has been under a lot of pressure but he has handled everything well so I was also pleased for him. He is a big motivator. He has passion for the game and it's easy working for him. For us, we don't think he gets angry. It's just the passion. He just loves the game so much."

VICTOR WANYAMA

"A lot of times what Neil has been doing or saying has been blown out of proportion as well. He will calm down in the future, you have to remember, he is not brand new but he has not been in the job too long. A lot of managers who have been in the job for a long time, they were a bit more passionate at the start of their career but then they mellow a bit."

JOHAN MJALLBY

Chapter 10: That's Entertainment

"I was delighted with the defensive record, it's what we work on with Woodsy. We did well last year as well, so we got the chance to beat that, and I was delighted with it. It's nice to see we kept on improving. It's all you can aim to do from one season to the next, just try and progress. I suppose that's one way you can judge yourself on how you had done at the end of the season. Woodsy has been brilliant, his coaching has been great. We identified things I needed to work on, and we've done that. Whether it's been in the gym, or yoga or whatever, you keep looking to make improvement."

FRASER FORSTER

"Fraser has been outstanding. He was brilliant in his first season but I think this time he was been even better. If you look at some of the games, the likes of Udinese away, I know we only drew that night but he's had some performances that have been world-class and he's been solid in every game."

ANTHONY STOKES

"The strikers work really hard closing down along with the Buchan graces the front cover of an Everton programme in 1981! midfielders, so it made our job easier and we have Fraser, who had been saving everything as well. We defend together. It starts from the front and everyone works together. We've done that well and we have a goal-keeper behind us who has been on fire, so that's why teams have found it difficult to score against us. That's the most important thing for the team, especially for us defenders, to have a guy in front of us who can pick up everything and make it difficult for the opponent. Victor and Beram usually play there and then you have Browny and Joe in front of us too, so they all make it hard for the other team to play through us and that was very important."

THOMAS ROGNE

"I had a chat with the manager at the start of the season and he wasn't happy with my consistency, but I know my body and I said that I need to have two or three games to find my rhythm, so he said that he would give me those games and it was up to me to keep myself in the team. And that's what I've done. Playing wide on the left-hand side is a position I like to play. It's the one I played when I was playing in Holland and also for the national team. For me it's easier to face the goal as I can beat people and I prefer to play there as a target man with my back to the goal. We have Gary Hooper and Stokesy who are good strikers and who score a lot of goals and I think I've found the right position."

GEORGIOS SAMARAS

Chapter 11: Glittering Prizes

"Obviously the manager is the one that brought me through. He had me in the reserves and gave me my chance to get on in the first team, and hopefully I've kicked on from there. Other managers might not have believed in me, but he put me on as soon as he could, and I just want to keep trying to get better. I was delighted in getting a few awards at the end of the season to show what I had done throughout the year. I got my chance and thought I would have played a good number of games, and then I was confident in my ability and confident in what I could do. I just want to go on and kick on and do the same next year."

JAMES FORREST

"It's been a good season for me. I've been happy with the way I have performed, even though there have been times where I felt I could have done better, but I have to be pleased with the way things went in Europe and in the league. The fans' support has been massive. I can't thank them enough in the way they stood by me. The things in my personal life have been bad, with my father passing away. The support they gave me was humbling and I can't thank them enough for that."

CHARLIE MULGREW

"I think James Forrest is the best young player in Scotland, and is in the top five young players in Britain."

GEORGIOS SAMARAS

"James Forrest in every training session and every game gets better and better. He works hard and is a good boy, a good person and a friendly person around the dressing room. He came in the first team the previous season and showed in his first season that he was good enough to play and do something for the club. This time he was much better, more experienced, scored goals, assisted goals, worked hard, and wanted to do everything for the team. With time he will become an even better player. He must just be focused and work hard. For me, he is one of the best players here."

BERAM KAYAL

"From what I've seen this season, in every game Charlie gets better. He's confident, he is quality on the ball and he's just a great player. He's technically good and just an all-round player."

KELVIN WILSON

"Charlie's probably one of the best centre-halves I've played with and he's versatile. He's also got a left foot to die for. His left peg really is dynamite. Anywhere from twenty to thirty yards out he's always going to put the keeper under pressure. On the ball, he's probably one of the most technical centre-halves about."

SCOTT BROWN

Chapter 12: Football Focus

"It had taken four years for the team and two for me as captain to get our hands on it – it had been too long but hopefully this is the start of something special. Lifting the trophy made it one of the biggest days of my life and I had been looking forward to it for four years. It meant even more because I was the captain and I think it's our turn to go on a wee run now. I lifted the Scottish Cup in 2011, and the other cups are good to win but the SPL is the one everyone wants. This is the big prize and it's the one that keeps everyone happy, the others are a bonus. We managed to make one of the biggest comebacks in history from fifteen points behind to being twenty points in front, so I don't think you will see that again."

SCOTT BROWN:

"After we won that day at Rugby Park I said I wanted to finish as top scorer. I needed one against Hearts, but in the end I got five, so it was a great end to the season. I maybe should have scored six! I had a couple of chances in the first half and then Paddy put a bit too much on the ball near the end. The only other time I scored five was when I was younger, in Sunday league football. We had to win the game. We knew the trophy was waiting for us and it was a good feeling. Scoring five goals, winning the game and getting the league trophy – you can't ask for much more than that. We won the league fair and square. We were fifteen points behind and if you take the ten points deduction away, it would still be ten points."

GARY HOOPER

"At the start of the season you aim to win the league and we have done that. It's the first time I have won it so obviously I was buzzing. It was good for all the lads and hopefully we can get more under our belt now. We have won it once now and we want to kick on and try and win more. It was a great honour for me, and it just showed where the team had come from – we had got better and better, and hopefully we can keep doing that. It was good to have played so many games and I was gutted to be injured and miss the last few games."

JAMES FORREST

"The Thai Tims were brilliant. I had watched them a few times on the computer and donated money to them. I think they are great and they really brightened up your day when you saw them. They are fantastic entertainment and you couldn't help but smile when they were around. Everybody here loves them and it was a great thing for them to come over."

MARK WILSON

"The fans are such a big part of the club, and they are known all over the world as being some of the best supporters. They have been constantly good throughout the season so it is hard to pick out one highlight, but every away ground we went to they packed it out. They stuck with us through thick and thin, even when things weren't going well – as they always do. They lifted us when things weren't really going well and gave us that boost. We were fifteen points behind at one point and at a lot of other clubs questions might have been asked, but they stuck with us and hopefully we rewarded them in the end with the league trophy."

ANTHONY STOKES

"There are a lot of good players for the future here. It's a massive phase in the development of these guys. Look at James Forrest. He's now classed as one of the first-team lads. We've got a really good set-up here with a few players ready to come in and play their part."

JOE LEDLEY

"Our average age is twenty-four so we have plenty more years left in us. If we keep this group of players together we will have a great chance of winning successive titles."

ADAM MATTHEWS

2011/12 Statistics

Scottish Premier League

July 24, 2011
Hibernian 0-2 Celtic
(Stokes, Ki)

Zaluska; M. Wilson, Loovens, K. Wilson, Izaguirre; Commons (Forrest 59), Ki, Kayal, Ledley; Hooper (Maloney 85), Stokes (Samaras 78)
Subs not used: Cervi, Mulgrew, Matthews, Wanyama

August 7, 2011
Aberdeen 0-1 Celtic
(Stokes)

Zaluska; Matthews, Majstorovic, K. Wilson, Izaguirre (Mulgrew 16);
Commons, Kayal, Ki, Ledley (Forrest 63); Hooper, Stokes
(Samaras 82)
Subs not used: Cervi, Samaras, Maloney, Wanyama, McCourt

August 13, 2011
Celtic 5-1 Dundee United
(Stokes, Hooper, Ki, Ledley, Forrest)

Zaluska; M. Wilson, Majstorovic, K. Wilson, Mulgrew; Brown, Ki,
Ledley, Commons (Forrest 63); Stokes (McCourt 77), Hooper
(Maloney 66)
Subs not used: Cervi, Matthews, Wanyama, Samaras

August 21, 2011
Celtic 0-1 St Johnstone

Forster; Matthews, Majstorovic, Wanyama, Mulgrew (M. Wilson 45);
Brown, Ki, Ledley (Forrest 74), Commons (McCourt 61); Maloney,
Stokes
Subs not used: Zaluska, Samaras, Cha, Murphy

August 28, 2011
St Mirren 0-2 Celtic
(Hooper 2)

Forster; Cha, Majstorovic, K. Wilson, Mulgrew; Brown, Ki
(Ledley 85), Kayal, Forrest; Stokes, Hooper
Subs not used: Zaluska, Matthews, Wanyama, Commons,
Samaras, Maloney

September 10, 2011
Celtic 4-0 Motherwell
(Forrest 2, Ledley, Ki)

Forster; Matthews, K. Wilson, Mulgrew, El Kaddouri; Forrest, Ki, Kayal (Wanyama 82), Ledley (Commons 70); Stokes (Bangura 67), Hooper
Subs not used: Zaluska, M. Wilson, Loovens, Samaras

September 18, 2011
Rangers 4-2 Celtic
(Hooper, El Kaddouri)

Forster; M. Wilson, K. Wilson, Loovens, El Kaddouri (Stokes 63); Brown (Forrest 75), Ki, Kayal, Mulgrew; Samaras (Bangura 83), Hooper
Subs not used: Zaluska, Matthews, Wanyama, Ledley

September 24, 2011
Celtic 2-0 Inverness Caley Thistle
(Ledley, Forrest)

Forster; Matthews, Majstorovic, Loovens, El Kaddouri; Forrest, Kayal, Ki (McCourt 75), Ledley; Stokes (Samaras 75) Hooper (Bangura 52)
Subs not used: Zaluska, Wanyama, M. Wilson, Rogne

October 2, 2011
Hearts 2-0 Celtic

Forster; Matthews (M. Wilson 73), Majstorovic, Mulgrew, El Kaddouri (McCourt 78); Forrest, Ki, Wanyama, Commons;

Bangura (Stokes 59), Hooper
Subs not used: Zaluska, Samaras, Rogne, Slane

October 10, 2011
Kilmarnock 3-3 Celtic
(Stokes 2, Mulgrew)

Forster; Cha (El Kaddouri 68), Majstorovic, Mulgrew, Matthews;
Forrest, Ki, Kayal (Wanyama 45), Ledley; Hooper (Bangura 45),
Stokes
Subs not used: Zaluska, M. Wilson, Rogne, Loovens

October 23, 2011
Celtic 2-1 Aberdeen
(Ki, Mulgrew)

Forster; Matthews, Loovens (Majstorovic 18), Mulgrew, Ledley; Kayal,
Wanyama (McCourt 72), Ki; Forrest; Hooper, Stokes
Subs not used: Zaluska, M. Wilson, El Kaddouri, Cha, McGeouch

October 29, 2011
Celtic 0-0 Hibernian

Forster; M. Wilson, Rogne, Mulgrew, Matthews; Forrest, Kayal
(Wanyama 33), Ledley, Ki (McCourt 70); Stokes, Hooper
(Samaras 84)
Subs not used: Zaluska, Cha, El Kaddouri, Majstorovic

November 6, 2011
Motherwell 1-2 Celtic
(Stokes, Hooper)

Forster; Cha, Majstorovic, Rogne, Matthews; Wanyama, Kayal;
Forrest (McGeouch 89), Commons (Hooper 62), Samaras
(McCourt 76); Stokes
Subs not used: Zaluska, Chalmers, Fraser, McGregor

November 19, 2011
Inverness Caley Thistle 0-2 Celtic
(Stokes 2)

Forster; Matthews, Wanyama, Majstorovic, El Kaddouri
(McCourt 69); Forrest (Commons 82), Kayal, Ledley, Samaras
(Ki 55); Hooper, Stokes
Subs not used: Zaluska, Fraser, McGeouch, F. Twardzik

November 23, 2011
Celtic 2-1 Dunfermline Athletic
(Hooper, Forrest)

Forster; Matthews, Wanyama, Majstorovic, Ledley; Forrest, Kayal, Ki,
Commons (McCourt 45); Hooper, Stokes (Samaras 79)
Subs not used: Zaluska, El Kaddouri, Blackman, Fraser, McGeouch

November 26, 2011
Celtic 5-0 St Mirren
(Hooper 3, Samaras, McGeouch)

Forster; Matthews, Majstorovic, Loovens, Ledley; Forrest
(McGeouch 65), Kayal, Wanyama, Samaras (Bangura 75); Hooper
(McCourt 74), Stokes
Subs not used: Zaluska, Ki, Blackman, El Kaddouri

December 4, 2011
Dundee United 0-1 Celtic
(Hooper)

Forster; Cha, Majstorovic, Loovens (Brown 67), Matthews; Forrest,
Kayal, Wanyama, Samaras; Hooper, Stokes (Ki 78)
Subs not used: Zaluska, Bangura, McCourt, McGeouch,
F. Twardzik

December 10, 2011
Celtic 1-0 Hearts
(Wanyama)

Forster; Cha, Loovens (Brown 46), Majstorovic, Mulgrew; Forrest,
Kayal, Wanyama, Samaras; Hooper, Stokes (Bangura 90+2)
Subs not used: Zaluska, K. Wilson, Ki, McGeouch, F. Twardzik

December 18, 2011
St Johnstone 0-2 Celtic
(Hooper, Ki)

Forster; Cha, Majstorovic (Rogne 33), Wanyama, Mulgrew; Brown,
Kayal (McGeouch77), Ki; Forrest, Hooper (Bangura 82), Samaras
Subs not used: Zaluska, Wilson, Blackman, F. Twardzik

December 24, 2011
Celtic 2-1 Kilmarnock
(Samaras 2)

Forster; Cha, Mulgrew, Wanyama; Ledley; Forrest (K. Wilson 49),

Brown, Kayal, Ki (Rogne 90); Hooper, Samaras (Bangura 66)
Subs not used: Zaluska, Izaguirre, McCourt, McGeouch

December 28, 2011
Celtic 1-0 Rangers
(Ledley)

Forster; Matthews, Rogne, Mulgrew, Ledley; Brown, Kayal, (Ki 77), Wanyama; Forrest; Hooper (Stokes 86), Samaras
Subs not used: Zaluska, Cha, Bangura, K. Wilson, McCourt

January 2, 2012
Dunfermline Athletic 0-3 Celtic
(Stokes, Wanyama, Mulgrew)

Forster; Matthews, Rogne, Mulgrew, Ledley; Forrest, Brown, Wanyama (Izaguirre 79), Samaras; Stokes, Hooper (Ki 66)
Subs not used: Zaluska, K. Wilson, Cha, McCourt, Bangura

January 14, 2012
Celtic 2-1 Dundee United
(Hooper, Wanyama)

Forster; Matthews, Rogne, Mulgrew, Izaguirre (Commons 77); Brown, Wanyama, Ledley, Samaras; Hooper, Stokes (Ki 65)
Subs not used: Zaluska, Cha, K. Wilson, McCourt, Keatings

January 21, 2012
St Mirren 0-2 Celtic
(Forrest, Brown)

Forster; Cha, Rogne, Mulgrew, Ledley; Brown, Wanyama, Ki
(Commons 57), Forrest (Matthews 87); Samaras (Stokes 57), Hooper
Subs not used: Zaluska, Izaguirre, K. Wilson, McGeouch

February 8, 2012
Hearts 0-4 Celtic
(Brown, Wanyama, Ledley, Hooper)

Forster; Matthews, Rogne (Majstorovic 63), K. Wilson, Mulgrew; Forrest,
Brown (Brozek 73), Wanyama, Ledley; Hooper (Stokes 66), Samaras
Subs not used: Zaluska, Cha, Ki, Commons

February 11, 2012
Celtic 1-0 Inverness Caley Thistle
(Ledley)

Forster; Matthews, Majstorovic, K. Wilson, Mulgrew; Forrest
(Commons 81), Brown, Wanyama, Ledley; Samaras, Hooper (Ki 64)
Subs not used: Zaluska, Cha, Stokes, Brozek, McCourt

February 19, 2012
Hibernian 0-5 Celtic
(Hooper 2, Stokes, Mulgrew, Ki)

Forster; Matthews, Rogne (Izaguirre 71), K. Wilson, Mulgrew;
Forrest, Brown, Wanyama (Ki 55), Ledley; Hooper (Commons 61),
Stokes
Subs not used: Zaluska, Samaras, Majstorovic, Brozek

February 22, 2012
Celtic 2-0 Dunfermline Athletic
(Mulgrew, Forrest)

Forster; Cha, K. Wilson, Mulgrew, Izaguirre (Forrest 67); Brown (Brozek 78), Ledley, Ki, Commons; Hooper, Stokes (Samaras 67)
Subs not used: Zaluska, Matthews, Majstorovic, McGeouch

February 25, 2012
Celtic 1-0 Motherwell
(Hooper)

Forster; Matthews, K. Wilson, Rogne, Mulgrew; Forrest (Commons 88), Wanyama (Stokes 59), Ki, Ledley; Hooper (Cha 76), Samaras
Subs not used: Zaluska, Majstorovic, Brozek, Izaguirre

March 3, 2012
Aberdeen 1-1 Celtic
(Stokes)

Forster; Lustig (Cha 68), Rogne, Wilson, Blackman (Wanyama 59); Forrest, Mulgrew, Ledley, Commons (McGeouch 66); Hooper, Stokes
Subs not used: Zaluska, McCourt, Loovens, Brozek

March 25, 2012
Rangers 3-2 Celtic
(Brown, Rogne)

Forster; Cha, Rogne, Mulgrew, Matthews; Brown, Wanyama, Ki (Commons 70), Ledley (Hooper 90), Samaras; Stokes (Izaguirre 29)

Subs not used: Zaluska, K. Wilson, McGeouch, Hooper, Brozek

April 1, 2012
Celtic 2-0 St Johnstone
(Samaras, Miller og)

Forster; Lustig (Matthews 55), Rogne, Loovens, Mulgrew; Commons, Brown, Ledley, Samaras; Stokes (Ki 63), Hooper (Blackman 87)
Subs not used: Zaluska, Izaguirre, K. Wilson, McGeouch

April 7, 2012
Kilmarnock 0-6 Celtic
(Mulgrew 2, Hooper 2, Loovens, Ledley)

Forster; Matthews, Loovens, K. Wilson, Mulgrew (Blackman 76); Brown (F. Twardzik 48), Ki, Ledley, Commons; Samaras (Stokes 74), Hooper
Subs not used: Zaluska, Cha, Brozek, Ibrahim

April 22, 2012
Motherwell 0-3 Celtic
(Watt 2, Cha)

Zaulska; Wanyama, Rogne, Mulgrew; Cha; Ki (McCourt 41), Commons (Lustig 77), Ledley, Izaguirre; Brozek (Watt 60), Hooper
Subs not used: Forster, Blackman, Stokes, Bangura

April 29, 2012
Celtic 3-0 Rangers
(Mulgrew, Commons, Hooper)

Forster; Matthews, Loovens, Mulgrew, Izaguirre; Brown, Wanyama, Ledley, Commons (McCourt 85); Samaras (Stokes 81), Hooper (Watt 89)
Subs not used: Zaluska, Cha, K. Wilson, McGeouch

May 3, 2012
Celtic 1-0 St Johnstone
(Stokes)

Zaluska; M. Wilson (Cha 76), Rogne, K. Wilson, Izaguirre; McGeouch (Hooper 70), Wanyama, Ledley, Commons (Ibrahim 76); Stokes, Bangura
Subs not used: Forster, Brozek, Lustig, Blackman

May 6, 2012
Dundee United 1-0 Celtic

Forster; Lustig, Rogne (Wanyama 55), Mulgrew; Matthews, Brown (McGeouch 71), Commons, Ledley, Izaguirre; Hooper, Stokes (Watt 45)
Subs not used: Zaluska, Bangura, Ibrahim, Cha

May 13, 2012
Celtic 5-0 Hearts
(Hooper 5)

Forster; Matthews, Loovens, Mulgrew; Wanyama; Brown (Kayal 67), Ledley (McCourt 69), Commons (Stokes 81), Izaguirre; Samaras, Hooper
Subs not used: Zaluska, Cha, Lustig, F. Twardzik

2011/12 Statistics

Scottish Cup

Round 4
January 8, 2012
Peterhead 0-3 Celtic
(Stokes 3)

Zaluksa; Cha, K. Wilson, Mulgrew (McGeouch 81) Izaguirre;
McCourt, Brown, Ki, Ledley (Wanyama 58); Stokes, Samaras
(F. Twardzik 71)
Subs not used: Forster, Wanyama, F. Twardzik, Matthews

Round 5
February 4, 2012

Inverness Caley Thistle 0-2 Celtic
(Samaras, Brown)

Forster; Matthews, K. Wilson, Rogne, Mulgrew; Brown, Wanyama, Ledley (F. Twardzik 90), Commons (Forrest 62); Hooper (Stokes 82), Samaras
Subs not used: Zaluska, Majstorovic

Quarter-final
March 11, 2012
Dundee United 0-4 Celtic
(Ledley, Samaras, Stokes, Brown)

Forster (Zaluska 89); Matthews, Rogne, Mulgrew, Ledley; Forrest, Wanyama, Brown, Samaras; Hooper (McCourt 82), Stokes (Commons 88)
Subs not used: Cha, K. Wilson

Semi-final
April 15, 2012
Celtic 1-2 Hearts
(Hooper)

Forster; Lustig (Wanyama 75), Loovens, K. Wilson, Mulgrew; Brown (McGeouch 82), Ki, Ledley, Commons; Samaras (Stokes 60), Hooper
Subs not used: Zaluska, Izaguirre

2011/12 Statistics

Scottish Communities League Cup

Round 3
September 21, 2011
Ross County 0-2 Celtic
(Hooper, Boyd og)

Forster; Matthews, Majstorovic, K. Wilson (Wanyama 46),
El Kaddouri; Forrest, Kayal, Ledley, Mulgrew; Stokes (Bangura 78),
Hooper (George 89)
Subs not used: Zaluska, Rogne

Quarter-final
October 26, 2011

Hibernian 1-4 Celtic
(Forrest 2, Stokes, Hooper)

Forster; Wilson, Rogne, Majstorovic, Matthews; Forrest (Cha 82), Kayal (Wanyama 70), Ki, Ledley; Stokes, Hooper (McCourt 77)
Subs not used: Zaluska, El Kaddouri

Semi-final
January 29, 2012
Celtic 3-1 Falkirk
(Stokes 2, Brown)

Forster; Cha (Matthews 68), Rogne, Mulgrew, Izaguirre (Ki 45); Forrest, Brown, Wanyama, Ledley; Hooper, Stokes (Commons 87)
Subs not used: Zaluska, Samaras

Final
March 18, 2012
Celtic 0-1 Kilmarnock

Forster, Matthews, Rogne (Ki 56), K. Wilson, Mulgrew; Forrest, Brown, Wanyama, Ledley (Commons 86); Stokes, Hooper (Samaras 80)
Subs not used: Cha, Zaluska

2011/12 Statistics

UEFA Europa League

Play-off round, first leg
August 18, 2011
Celtic 0-0 FC Sion

Forster; Cha, Majstorovic, Mulgrew, M. Wilson; Brown, Ki, Ledley, Commons (Forrest 56); Stokes (Samaras 69), Samaras (McCourt 85)
Subs not used: Zaluska, Matthews, Wanyama, Slane

Play-off round, second leg
August 25, 2011
FC Sion 3-1 Celtic
(Mulgrew)

Forster; Cha, K. Wilson, Majstorovic, Mulgrew; Brown, Kayal (Forrest 72), Ki, Ledley (Commons 88); Samaras, Hooper

Subs not used: Zaluska, M. Wilson, Matthews, McCourt, Stokes

Group I, matchday 1
September 15, 2011
Atletico Madrid 2-0 Celtic

Forster; M. Wilson (Matthews 78), Loovens, K. Wilson, Mulgrew;
Forrest (Commons 82), Ki, Kayal, Ledley (Bangura 77), Samaras;
Hooper
Subs not used: Zaluska, Wanyama, F. Twardzik, George

Group I, matchday 2
September 29, 2011
Celtic 1-1 Udinese
(Ki)

Zaluska; Matthews, Majstorovic, Mulgrew, Ledley (M. Wilson 46);
Wanyama; Ki, Kayal; Forrest (Samaras 72); Bangura, Hooper
Subs not used: Forster, Loovens, McCourt, F. Twardzik, Stokes

Group I, matchday 3
October 20, 2011
Rennes 1-1 Celtic
(Ledley)

Forster; Matthews, Loovens, Mulgrew, Ledley; Kayal, Wanyama;
Cha, Ki (Bangura 89), Forrest; Stokes
Subs not used: Zaluska, Majstorovic, M. Wilson, McCourt,
George, McGregor

Group I, matchday 4
November 3, 2011
Celtic 3-1 Rennes
(Stokes 2, Hooper)

Forster; Cha, Loovens (Fraser 46), Majstorovic, Matthews; Kayal,
Wanyama; Forrest (Hooper 79), McCourt (Commons 66), Samaras;
Stokes
Subs not used: Zaluska, George, Chalmers, McGregor

Group I, matchday 5
November 30, 2011
Celtic 0-1 Atletico Madrid

Forster; Matthews, Majstorovic, Loovens, Ledley (Mulgrew 38);
Kayal, Wanyama (Hooper 45), Forrest, Ki, Samaras; Stokes
(Brown 75)
Subs not used: Zaluska, Bangura, McCourt, F. Twardzik

Group I, matchday 6
December 15, 2011
Udinese 1-1 Celtic
(Hooper)

Forster; Cha, Majstorovic, Wanyama, Mulgrew; Brown, Kayal
(Stokes 70), Ki; Forrest, Samaras (Bangura 83); Hooper
Subs not used: Zaluska, K. Wilson, Toshney, George, F. Twardzik